I0068186

TAKE BACK YOUR CAREER

HOW TO PLAY TODAY'S CAREER GAME

" The best way to predict the future is to invent it. " —ALAN KAY

JAN MARINO

Copyright © 2011 Jan Marino

All rights reserved. Except as permitted under the U.S. Copyright Act of 1976, no part of this publication may be reproduced, distributed, or transmitted in any form or by any means, or stored in a database or retrieval system, without the prior written permission of the publisher.

1421 Press
1670 Valencia Way
Mundelein, IL 60060

1421 Press name and logo are trademarks of Round Table Companies and Writers of the Round Table Inc.

Front cover design by Nathan Brown
Interior design and layout by Sunny B. DiMartino

Printed in the United States of America

First Edition: July 2011
10   9   8   7   6   5   4   3   2   1

Library of Congress Cataloging-in-Publication Data

Marino, Jan
Take Back Your Career: How to Play Today's Career Game / Jan Marino.—
1st ed. p. cm.
ISBN 978-1-937443-01-6
1. Success in business.   2. Personal growth.   I. Title.

To John with all my love.

—Jan

TABLE OF CONTENTS

INTRODUCTION

IN MAY OF 1990, I WAS LAID OFF FOR THE FIRST TIME IN MY CAREER. That was my introduction to the world of career transition—a world I have experienced three times since then. I wish I could say that with each merger or downsizing, it got easier... but it didn't. What I can say is that each time was different. Each time, I learned something new about myself—and the process of job hunting and career management. And each time, I kept saying, "There has to be a better way."

For the past five years, I've been on a mission to discover a better process for managing my career. I decided that one way to learn what was needed to devise a better process was to volunteer at the local community career center. I've also been a senior advisor and consultant to major outplacement firms. I've coached over fifteen hundred people who were searching for new jobs. I've learned so much from all of them, but one client in particular has always stuck with me.

Tim was a COO who told me that he wanted to "get back in the game." He was tired of being on the bench. He said the longer he was out of the game, the more the game changed and he wasn't in the thick of it. I didn't understand what he meant until he explained that, for him, work and career were THE ultimate competition sport. He saw it as a competitive game where you had to stay in shape, continuously work your game plans, scout out the competition, know the field of play, and, above all, craft your winning plays.

Tim was so right in his sports analogy of career management. Once I started looking at the process from a competitive, contact sports angle it became obvious that the disciplines needed for sports are also necessary when managing your career. When you start to understand this concept, you see that you want to be able to lead and play on a team, remain marketable in a competitive environment, and develop and execute game-winning plays.

So, what happens when you look at career management as THE ultimate contact sport? First, you declare that you want to get into the game and win! Then you want to know the following:

— How the game has changed
— What the playing field looks like
— The rules
— How to form your winning team
— What tools you'll be using
— How to get into peak shape
— What plays you'll run
— How to keep up a winning streak

I'm writing this book to give you a better understanding of the new career management game. Because here's the thing: Everything about this contact sport has changed in the last few years. There are new rules, new playing fields, new team members, new competition. I've always believed that learning a new sport from an expert is crucial; for this game, I'll be your coach. This book is your playbook. It will supply you with the necessary information, exercises, and examples to guide you in creating your personalized career management game plan. You're closer to a breakthrough career than you think.

Ready? Game on!

CHAPTER ONE

THE NEW CAREER GAME

" If you don't know where you're going, you will wind up somewhere else. " —YOGI BERRA

WHAT IS THE CAREER GAME?

The career management game is one of the most competitive sports you'll ever play. It tests your commitment to your goals and, most importantly, your commitment to yourself. When you develop the confidence and courage to fully participate in your career by deciding who you are and what you have to offer, you're a winning player!

Now, this is what's happened to the career management game: The rules, playing field, team members, competition, and game plays have changed. And there was no big announcement, so most of us missed it.

WHAT THE GAME USED TO BE

The career game used to involve growing up on the job, working at one or two companies throughout your entire career. I have a good friend who went to work for a bank the summer she graduated from high school. Thirty-two years later, she's still at the same bank. She started as a teller and worked her way up through the ranks to a vice president position. She's worked in the consumer, commercial, administrative, and technology divisions of the organization, surviving five major mergers. This type of situation is almost unheard of these days!

Under the old rules, you followed a similar path as my banking friend. You remained with the same organization for at least ten to fifteen years, every so often creating a resume reflecting your responsibilities and title. Just for practice, you sent it out in response to ads you found in the newspaper. If you got laid off or fired, you could use the techniques you learned when you first started your career to find a new job. You could call a few old friends, for example, to let them know you were in the market. By tapping into a close network, you could usually land a new position in a matter of weeks.

John, a client of mine, assumed that today's career game is the same as it was years ago. He was thrown into the job market when his company restructured, eliminating his position as a call center manager. Confident he would quickly find a new position, John took a couple months off to complete projects around his house. When he decided to get back into job-search mode, he discovered that the market was much tighter and more competitive than he'd thought. He also discovered how weak his network was. In the end, it took John fourteen months to find a position comparable to the one he'd lost. He now realizes that he could have used his time much more productively by focusing on his search and learning how to play the new career game.

WHEN THE GAME CHANGED—AND WHY

The game started to change in the late 1980s, when globalization hit American businesses and companies began merging. Suddenly, companies had to compete in a world where other countries could produce goods and services cheaper and sometimes better. Productivity and cost became the priority, and loyalty and longevity were out. What this means to employees is that companies will no longer "take care of us" or play the part of a work family. Companies are in business to make money and produce dividends for shareholders. In many cases, we are the shareholders, and we demand profits. Interesting dilemma, huh?

——————— WHAT THE CAREER GAME LOOKS LIKE TODAY

The new career game is a contact sport. It's a game with varied playing fields, positions, and competitors, and requires mastery of the rules, team selection, and workouts.

The changes in the career game probably aren't noticeable to most people until they find themselves in the job market. That's when many inadvertently discover the biggest change: WE are responsible for our careers. We can't turn to a search firm or an outplacement firm and say, "Get me another job." We can't just look through the newspaper every Sunday and answer job postings. Today's career game requires a focused, strategic plan that is continuously followed and then revised when needed. And that plan starts with building knowledge.

——————————————— THE PLAYING FIELD

The fields for different sports include artificial turf, natural grass, ice, wood, gravel, water, or asphalt. They are smooth, bumpy, round, straight, hilly, choppy, wide, or narrow, and for any player, understanding the field is a crucial part of the game.

The old career playing field was relatively simple. At its widest, it encompassed a few states or even Europe. But for most of us, the field was local, easy to find, and recognizable. We did our jobs near our home or at least in the same city. For instance, my father owned a pharmacy. He walked to work most mornings and opened the store, which was four blocks from our house. If he had deliveries to make during the day, he might take the car. While our new house was being built in the 1950s, we lived in an apartment over the store. He had the same staff for years, so there wasn't much turnover. The nearest competition was twenty miles away. My father owned his playing field and was in total control.

On the old playing field, you played the same position. You mastered your talents and the plays you needed to make. Players didn't change much unless someone was promoted, retired, or died. It was a badge of honor to have worked for the same organization for twenty-five years or more. I saw a sign in the front window of our local grocery store indicating that one of the employees was being honored for twenty-eight years of service. That used to be the norm—our careers were measured in decades at the same company. It was an accomplishment.

Today, the average American stays at one job for three to five years, and that timeframe is getting shorter, because employees feel no loyalty to employers. If you've been with the same organization for more than ten years, you'll want to be prepared to tell the market why your strategy to stay put was a good decision and what you contributed by staying. If your answer to why you stayed is that it was an easy commute, that isn't going to sell you in this new market. On the flip side, if you've been at three companies in the last five years, be prepared to explain why you changed jobs so often. The stigma of "job hopping" hasn't disappeared.

The biggest change in the playing field is this: *It is wherever you are.* Think about it. Technology allows us to have offices everywhere; the field has no physical constraints. We are no longer confined to buildings, cubes, and conference rooms. We conduct business from our car, home, soccer field, gym, sidewalk café, or almost any place you can imagine. One of my clients manages a sales team with locations in Chicago, Los Angeles, New York, Paris, New Delhi, and Hong Kong. He's on conference calls at all hours. For some people, this concept is a huge challenge because the job creeps into personal space and family life. But putting boundaries on when and where you work is also part of the new playing field.

THE POSITIONS

More than the field has changed in the new career game. Our positions, too, have been redefined. We're no longer confined to traditional, full-time roles with the expected accompanying packages. There are many lucrative options available to the savvy player, including part-time contractor positions, consultant positions, and opportunities to become an entrepreneur. You'll begin to start thinking "out of the box" as you explore new opportunities.

THE TOOLS

Today's game-winning tools are both high-tech and surprisingly low-tech.

When it comes to technology, realize that you will be using different media (if you aren't already) than in years past. In addition to meeting, networking, and interviewing face-to-face or by phone, you might be using video, panel interviews, and social media such as LinkedIn, Twitter, Facebook, and blogs. When it comes to interviews, most of us are better at face-to-face meetings, but today you will likely have several phone interviews before you shake anyone's hand.

Next, understand that you will be expected to "hit the ground running" in a new position, which means acting as if you've been there forever. You're expected to be a quick study and get to know the culture and your teammates very quickly. You're expected to read the office politics just as fast. To meet these challenges head-on, prioritizing our interpersonal skills is a must.

My ninety-two-year-old aunt recently commented that she felt the art of writing letters and carrying on a conversation with real people in real time was being lost because of the Internet. She said that we have more gadgets than ever for communicating but that the quality of our communications has suffered. While the Internet has opened up new avenues of communicating (families stay in touch on Facebook; professionals network on LinkedIn; we can all find a voice through blogging), I do agree that we have to work harder on interpersonal skills... especially listening.

Listening is a tool that is often neglected in today's career game. I've taught courses on listening skills, and it always amazes me how difficult real listening is. Try listening to a coworker and not interrupting. Let him finish his comments, and try to listen for what he's really saying by watching his body language. You'll notice that your mind will race ahead, and you'll want to finish his sentences or jump in with your opinion. If you're really not interested in what he's saying, you'll probably mentally check out all together. However, if we don't listen carefully, we miss out on chances to discover opportunities for ourselves.

Becoming a good listener can give you another advantage on the playing field. Your competition may present solutions that won't work because they didn't understand the real needs. By becoming an effective listener, you'll be in a position to offer valid, valuable solutions—and thus set yourself apart from the pack. If you're interested in learning more about listening skills, you might pick up *Listening: The Forgotten Skill: A Self-Teaching Guide,* by Dennis Kratz.

THE COMPETITION

In the new career game, competition comes at us from all directions. In the United States, there are four generations in the workforce. In When Generations Collide, Lynne Lancaster and David Stillman address who the generations are and why they clash. They define the four generations: Traditionalists, Baby Boomers, Generation Xers, and Millennials.

Traditionalists were born between 1900 and 1945. They number about seventy-five million. Baby Boomers number eighty million and were born between 1946 and 1964. Generation Xers were born between 1965 and 1980, and are the smallest group at forty-six million. Millennials were born between 1981 and 1999 and number seventy-six million.

Because of this diversity in generations, there's a good chance that those of us over forty-five will be working for someone in his or her thirties. That's why the concept of ageless thinking is so important today. (Not easy, but important.) As you manage your career, you want to turn every interaction into a learning event. Learn everything you can from and about your competition—no matter their age.

For instance, I recently was hired to help a newly graduated MBA student plan her career for the next five years. She wanted to brand herself and learn how to network better so she could network her way into a new job. We learned an important lesson pretty quickly into our business relationship: I preferred phone calls and face-to-face meetings, while my client preferred texting and emails. Each time she would send questions or comments, she sent them via email or text. I wanted to talk ideas out with her so I could observe her reactions. Through several text messages, we agreed to divide our communication preferences. I agreed to email and text more and she agreed to pick up the phone occasionally. This is one instance of how generational differences can affect communication preferences. Though this example happens to be of a client, the same differences can be applied to competition and hiring managers. Not paying attention to the way our communication styles differed could have damaged our relationship. In a career transition, it could cost you a job.

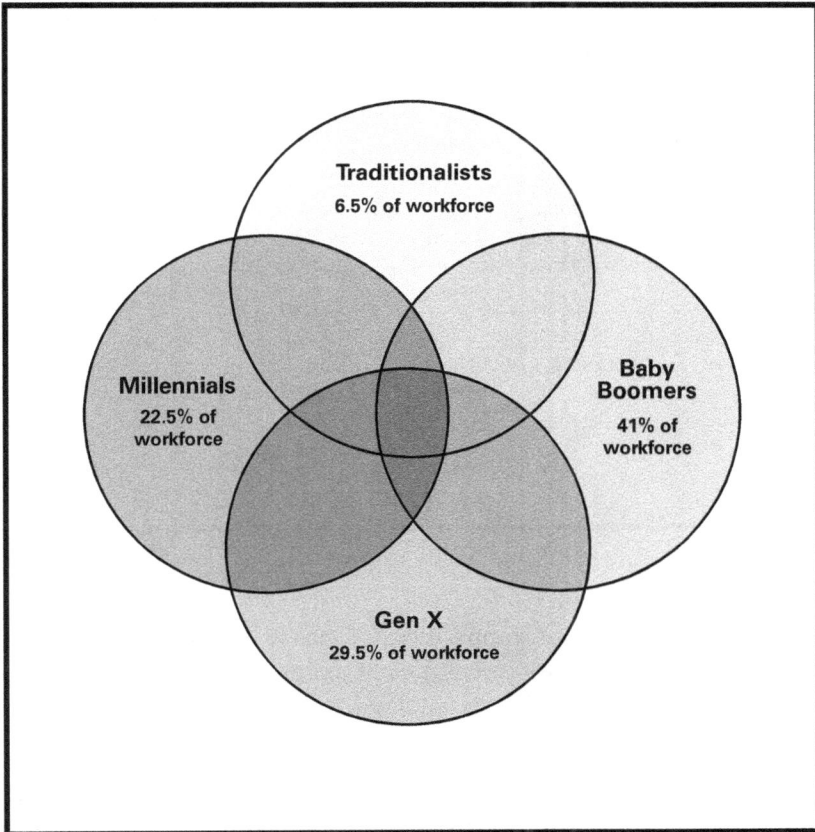

Traditionalists
6.5% of workforce

Millennials
22.5% of workforce

Baby Boomers
41% of workforce

Gen X
29.5% of workforce

Take a look at this table and determine which generation you fall into. This comparison chart is very helpful because it illuminates how the different generations operate and what elements drive them.

	Traditionalists	Baby Boomers	Generation X	Millennials
Core values	Respect for authority; conformation; discipline	Optimism; involvement	Skepticism; fun; informality	Realism; confidence; fun, fun, fun
Financial habits	Save-for-rainy-day; pay cash	Buy now, pay later	Conservative; savers	Earn to buy; in debt from student loans
Communications tools	One-on-one memos	Touch-tone phones; open communication style	Cell phones; don't call me at home	Internet; smart phones; emails
Work drivers	Dedicated; hard-working; "company man"	Ambitious; driven; need to succeed in business	Balance in business life and home life	Optimistic; high degree of self reliance
Personal drivers	Follow rules; don't need instant gratification	Optimistic; belief in personal growth	Global thinkers; self-reliant; open to new technology; less formal	Strong morals; very community-minded

—FDU Magazine

Understanding your competition for jobs will continue to be a key to successfully managing your career. As always, knowledge is power. Businesses have problems that need to be solved, and it's up to you to explain how your expertise benefits them. Decide how you want to position yourself in this arena. How do your accomplishments and talents help level the field in your favor and set you apart from the competition?

——————————— DEFINING YOUR PLAYING FIELD

In order to effectively navigate your present field, you need to define it. By that, I mean take time to clearly understand your environment. What has changed in the last year? Is your organization ripe for a merger or takeover? Has your company introduced new products or services? What is your career track? How are you positioned? These questions are just as relevant if you've been laid off; the clearer you can get about your present situation, the easier it is to plan for changes.

So that you can get a good picture of your ideal playing field, complete these exercises. These activities will also help you figure out how you can be more productive, because where you work is an important element in your successful game plan.

Begin this exercise by listing criteria for your playing field: distance from home; method of getting to work (train, bus, car); location (city, suburbs, home); environment (e.g., large office building); position; etc.

Now, with your criteria in mind, choose and research twenty companies you're interested in working for; complete the following table.

——————————— SAMPLE ———————————

Who: Target Companies	What: Industries	Why: You Chose the Company	Where: Location

Who: Target Companies	What: Industries	Why: You Chose the Company	Where: Location

CAREER PLAYBOOK

The career game today demands flexibility and courage. You've started positioning yourself in this fast-paced environment by learning how the career game and field have changed—and you've done the important work of beginning to define your own present and ideal career playing field. The next chapter will spell out the ten new rules to make this knowledge work for you.

CHAPTER TWO

THE NEW RULES

" The will to win is important, but the will to prepare is vital. " —JOE PATERNO

I MET MY CLIENT, Vince, for the first time at a networking event in 2010. He had that deer in the headlights look about him as he shyly introduced himself. It was painful to listen to him stammer through his qualifications; I didn't know anyone could blush that many colors of red. He told the group that his specialty was "utilizing geographical analysis to develop corporate strategy." None of us had any idea what that meant and no one asked. The meeting broke up, and I ran into Vince in the parking lot. I asked him exactly what his profession was, hoping I'd get a better description—and this time I did. He explained that he used geographic information and demographics to select store sights of his company (i.e., where to put the next McDonald's, Walgreens, or Costco).

Vince had just been laid off, and this was the first time he'd looked for a job since college. He said this was the first networking event he'd ever attended, and he was very uncomfortable introducing himself to people he didn't know. He leaned against his car, shaking his head, and said that he was highly regarded in his industry, but he'd been in the job market for three months and still hadn't gotten an interview. He said people kept telling him that the rules had changed for a job search, but he couldn't get a handle on what the new rules were.

Several of my clients tell a very similar story as Vince did about today's market. They talk about outdated rules in the job search process. They share their feelings of alienation and humiliation because of job loss or stalled careers, and confess that they thought their jobs were safe from elimination. They admit they hadn't cultivated business connections, and their resumes were several years out of date. Most of them don't know how to use social networking or how to create a personal brand. Selling themselves was a new concept. Until they lost their job, they believed that the workplace contract between an individual and an organization was still alive.

The rules for managing your career in today's market have changed dramatically. What's more, they will continue to change. Fortunately, you've already begun positioning yourself in the playing field, so you're in a prime spot to start practicing the rules of the new career game. I've identified these rules by the work I've done guiding hundreds of clients over the last six years. They're real-world and practical, and incorporating them into your career game plan will take you to new successes.

Ready? Let's go!

—— 1. A DYNAMIC MARKET PRESENCE IS AN IMPERATIVE

As you've already learned, your **personal brand** sets the tone for who you are and how you are perceived in the marketplace. It is an emotional response by your target audience to you: what they *think* about you, what they *say* about you, how they categorize you, what "box" they put you in. Your personal brand is also how YOU think of yourself. If you don't give yourself credit for your accomplishments, no one else will. Forget what your mom and your teachers told you about bragging. This is the time to stand up straight, throw your chest out, and be proud of yourself! This is also the time to put your pride into words.

THE NEW RULES

From now on, you must see yourself as THE PRODUCT, and you are your number one salesperson. You're probably saying to yourself, "I'm not in sales." Or "I don't know anything about sales." Not true! Every time you've persuaded someone to go along with your ideas or projects, you were selling. When you convinced your family to go to the Black Hills on vacation, you were selling. You've been selling your whole life but probably never thought about it. AND you're really good at it. What's more, you know the product you're selling better than anyone, which will take your skills to a whole new level.

2. THE NEW CAREER GAME REVOLVES AROUND NETWORKING MORE THAN EVER...

...both face-to-face (called human networking—don't you love it!) and social networking (online networking). It's all about who you know and how well you're connected. The "what you know" is a given because competition is stiff, so you'd better know your stuff. The "who you know" (networking) is one of the most misunderstood plays in the career game. The key to growing an effective and productive network is to give more than you get; it's about helping others solve their problems. When you meet someone new, listen to his needs and think about who you know that could get him closer to his goal.

Here's the secret about networking—you don't keep score. In other words, just because you help someone or connect them to someone else doesn't necessarily mean that they will return the favor. And that's okay, because you want to establish yourself as a resource for people. Keeping score is hard work and a waste of time. Your goal is to build a reputation as a resource for people and as a person who's connected. You also want to be known as a giver, not a taker. Always being a "taker" isn't a smart playing strategy.

People always ask, "How do I start building a human network?" You start by knowing who you are, what you want, and how people can help you. It's important that you know how people can help you but NOT asking if they know who is hiring or if they can help you find a job. Either one of those questions scares the listener off because he doesn't want to think about the possibility that he, too, could be in the job search process. Try to start the conversation by introducing yourself and finding out about *him*.

So, here's the formula for starting a conversation and beginning to build a network. First,use a simple introduction. "Hi, my name is John Marino." Don't get into details yet. The other person will usually tell you her name and you'll shake hands. (Remember to use a firm handshake.) Next, ask her a question such as, "How often do you attend these kinds of meetings?" Or ask about her business: "How long have you been in your industry?" You're trying to establish some commonality with the other person.

The next step is to let the other person know that you're in a career transition and you're expanding your network. Offer your card and explain that you want to add her to your network. Usually, the other person will give you her card in return. Now the way is open to explore how you two can help each other. Explain what kinds of people you want to connect with and ask what the other person needs help with. With this approach, you both get the information you want. If the other person is reluctant to helping you, simply thank her and break off the conversation. You'll get better at figuring who's a good contact for you as you practice your approach at more networking events. Your goal is to spend time with people who are open to networking and helping you connect with key people within your industry. You can also focus on organizations you want to network into by asking people if they know anyone at that organization and whether they would be open to introducing you. For example, a friend of mine is looking for a position as an executive director for a non-profit. She asked me if I knew an executive director she could connect with, and I made two email introductions to my contacts in the non-profit world. Building a network of contacts you trust, and being a trustworthy contact yourself, is one of the most important rules of the new career game.

3. RESUMES ARE OVERRATED

We spend entirely too much time on them. Finalizing your resume can be a never-ending process if you let it. Focus on key elements: make your accomplishments measurable; use keywords from the job posting if you're responding to a posted position; make certain that you have no spelling or grammar errors; and update your resume every six months. If you're in the job market, spending three weeks perfecting your resume isn't going to get you out on the playing field or in a better playing position. That's why I won't spend any more time on resumes in this playbook. There are lots of books already written about how to create one, so I won't re-invent the wheel. Give yourself a week to create a resume you can live with and then run with it!

4. COMPETITION IS FIERCE

You might say this is a given. However, as with any sport, knowing and understanding the competition is an important part of being a winner.

The generational competition is heating up as baby boomers defer retirement because they can't afford or don't want to retire. Meanwhile, employees are becoming more educated globally. Get to know your competition by reading articles about your career industry and acquainting yourself with others who are looking for jobs similar to your target job. One way to do this is by attending job clubs at your local career center. Members of these groups come from different industries, but there are always several from the same field. When job seekers attend these meetings, they come face-to-face with their competition. This type of forum offers a non-threatening environment in which you can learn what your competitors are thinking and how they represent themselves. This can give you a crucial advantage as you learn how to differentiate yourself from them in the market.

5. YOU WILL HAVE MANY CAREERS AND JOBS IN YOUR LIFETIME

I had a great model for how to maneuver through multiple jobs and careers. My dad started his career as a carpenter and builder. He was also a painter and a business owner. After World War II, he used the

GI bill and went to pharmacy school. He was almost forty went he got his pharmacy diploma. That was 1949, and having multiple careers was uncommon. Today, having several jobs and many careers is becoming the standard. Daniel Pink's Free Agent Nation outlines the trend of many careers—namely, as companies cut back on benefits and retirement programs, people will be needing multiple income streams.

6. YOU ARE RESPONSIBLE FOR YOURSELF AND YOUR CAREER

This may sound like a common sense statement, and it is. However, the tendency to let others make career decisions for us still persists. Clients tell me they want to work for a company for the rest of their career, and they hope they never have to be in the job market again. But because companies will continue to merge and new companies will be forming, taking responsibility for keeping yourself marketable is essential. You do this by knowing what's going on in your industry and staying on top of who's doing what. It also means getting involved in industry associations and trying to keep current on industry trends. When you **keep yourself marketable,** you take control of your career; you call the plays. The days of coasting on the job are gone. That's why an active network keeps you in the game.

7. KNOW WHAT VALUE YOU BRING TO THE MARKETPLACE

Do your homework: Know what an organization needs and how you can solve its problems. Companies are looking for people who think on their feet to solve issues. Once you are clear about your value and contributions, you are in a place of power. Look at your accomplishments and note what strategies you used to solve problems. Figure out how your contributions impacted the bottom line of an organization. Start to think in terms of, "I've orchestrated successes for ABC Company, and I'll bring the same successes to your company!"

8. ARROGANCE AND CONFIDENCE ARE NOT THE SAME THING

Know the difference. Confident people are happy in their skin. You own your accomplishments and talents, and you are honest about who you are. Confidence shows up as being tolerant of other views. Confidence is knowing that you are successful and that, although you may face setbacks, you are a winner. Confidence gives you the courage to take risks, follow your instincts, and allow your talents to take you to the goal line. When you start to doubt yourself, stop that voice in your head and recall one of your biggest accomplishments. Doubt creates fear and second-guessing, which hinders your performance. Meditating and quieting your mind for ten minutes daily helps you retain confidence. Continuing to produce results and reaching your goals, of course, makes your confidence soar.

9. YOU ARE NOT WHAT YOU DO

Remember this rule. Chances are that at some point in your career, you will be laid off. Just because you lose your job doesn't mean that you lose your experiences, talents, ideas, leadership, and determination. You are NOT your job, so don't lose your identity in it. Don't treat your job like a security blanket that you can hide under to avoid change and challenges. Keep your brand and your network up to date.

10. RETIREMENT IS BEING REDEFINED

Either for financial reasons or because we want to, we are all working longer. The idea of retiring when I'm sixty-five is foreign to me. I plan to be working for another twenty-five years, which is at least another two or three careers. You may not want to think about it, but chances are good that you'll live longer than you imagined you would. That will you give several additional years to contribute to the workplace.

Now that you have a better understanding of the rules used in to-day's career game, you'll be a real competitor. For further practice in defining your goals and developing your career strategy, take some time to complete the following exercises. Getting clarity about your values and how you contribute help you take back your career because you are tapping into what is important to you and why you make the choices you make. These activities help you get out of "auto" mode and into "conscience" mode. This is a call to become active and take charge of your life and career.

EXERCISES

1 List your top ten values.

2 Write one or two sentences about how each value contributes to your life and career.

3 Write three value statements for yourself: "I bring value by..."

4 Describe what you want your legacy to be. Why is it important to you?

5 What need do you fill in the marketplace?

6 Who is your target audience, and what are their three biggest needs?

7 How will you address their needs?

8 Set a goal to add two people to your network each week. The easiest way to start is to get back in contact with people you used to work with but haven't spoken with in the last six months. Make a list of potential contacts and send them an email, telling them that you're reconnecting with valued colleagues and that you'll be calling them to catch up.

THE NEXT STEPS

Now that you understand the new rules of the game, you're in the ideal position to learn how to craft your personal vision and mission statements. The next chapter will explain why these statements are crucial to taking ownership of your career management. You will also learn how to create your personal brand and establish a network that will give you an advantage in the career game for the rest of your life.

CHAPTER THREE

YOUR PERSONAL VISION AND MISSION

" *My motto was always to keep swinging. Whether I was in a slump or feeling badly or having trouble off the field, the only thing to do was keep swinging.* **"** —HANK AARON

PEOPLE who have never lost a job because of downsizing don't understand the trauma of the experience. They don't know how humiliating and demoralizing it is. Because we identify ourselves by what we do for a living, losing our job can mean that we lose *ourselves*.

I speak from personal experience. When I got laid off in 1995, my working colleagues didn't know how to help, and I didn't know what kind of help I needed. All I knew was that I needed a JOB. I was panicked and scared. I spent hours on my resume and was angry with my situation. My fear and negative energy hit people the minute they met me, and it was hard for friends and relatives to help me. I had *stinkin' thinkin'*.

I was frustrated and bitter, and these emotions became more pronounced as I searched for a new position. I wasn't making any headway and began feeling sorry for myself. Finally, a good friend pulled me aside and explained that she didn't know or like this defeated, whiney person I'd become. That was my "snap out of it!" moment. I realized that I needed to change my thoughts and actions or I would never get out of my rut.

Creating this book is a great vehicle for me to share what I've learned from my own experiences and those of hundreds of coaching clients over the last ten years. I learned, for example, that I didn't have to go through my job search alone. I learned that people want to help, but you have to know what you want first; asking someone if she knows of any job openings isn't the best way to find out what's available. I learned that resumes are vastly overrated. I learned that the competition is fierce and that I had to keep learning so I could keep up. I learned that I needed to be very clear about what I wanted and why I was filling a market need. The most value lesson I've learned is that I now know how to market myself and show the value I bring to the table. How to market myself and show the value I bring to the table. And that all started with determining my personal career vision and mission.

——————————————————— ELLEN'S STORY ↘

Here is a good example of what can happen when you decide to be a player. Ellen is a financial analyst with ten years of experience working for a major bank. She coasted through the first few years of her job with no real thought about where she was going or what she really wanted from her career. She got a wake-up call when rumors started circulating that the bank she was working for was about to be merged with another organization. Worse, analysts at the other organization were doing exactly the kinds of projects Ellen was working on. She realized her job could be in jeopardy.

The merger was completed and Ellen didn't lose her position, but she started to understand the need to become more involved in planning her career; she needed to be much more proactive with her network so that she knew what was happening in her industry. She also wanted to become more marketable and establish a reputation for being a reliable resource for others, so she set a goal to meet four new people a week and keep track of who these contacts were, how she could help them, and vice versa.

Within six months, Ellen had expanded her network from twenty to two-hundred connections, all of whom she actually met through the phone or in person. She developed her mission and vision statements and began a branding strategy. She joined a professional association for financial analysts and became involved in the membership team. This gave her exposure to her peers and helped her stay updated on industry trends.

Like Ellen prior to the merger, many of us go through our careers without thinking about where we're going or why. We let circumstances dictate what our career looks like. When the economy is good and jobs are plentiful, we have lots of choices and can fall into complacency. However, when times get tough, we're not prepared for our options being limited—or eliminated. One day we get laid off, and we have no idea what to do next.

The trick is to create a plan and vision for your career now. It's never too late or too early. Once you have your vision and mission, you can win in the new world of work because you know what you want.

YOUR CAREER VISION STATEMENT

What do you choose to make your life's work stand for? Answering this question helps you stay focused on your destination and guides you to identifying your unique achievements and contributions.

EXERCISE: 30 MINUTES

Sit in a calm, quiet place and think about what you want to achieve in your career and why that goal is important to you. Where do you see yourself in your career now and in the future? Give yourself enough time to think it through and decide what's important. Write down the thoughts that come to you. List them out so you can see them. Writing will help you own your vision, because you've taken it from the idea state to the written state. Describing your vision in words gives it more

YOUR PERSONAL VISION AND MISSION

power, which will lead to action. Remember, there is no right or wrong way to complete this exercise. This is YOUR vision of YOUR career.

As an example of this process, a recent client of mine had just been promoted into the first position where he felt he could make a real impact on the company. His first step to creating a career vision statement was to list nouns and descriptors he wanted to embody, such as *leader, good listener,* and *customer-focused.* He then made a list of what roles he wanted for himself. He saw himself as a leader in his field. He could implement programs to increase customer satisfaction. He also wanted to be better than the competition. Armed with these adjectives and roles, he came up with two versions of his vision statement:

> **Vision Statement #1:** "I will become a leader in the financial services industry, ensuring that our services are superior to our competitors'. I will listen to our customers and include their suggestions to increase client satisfaction."

> **Vision Statement #2:** "I will be a new breed of human resource AND financial service professional. I will be a nationally known and respected expert because I will educate corporations on how they can integrate these two disciplines to their competitive advantage."

Read your vision statement out loud and see how it feels. You may want to tweak it a couple of times, but chances are good that you'll get it right the first time.

YOUR CAREER MISSION STATEMENT

Once you understand your vision, you can create your career mission statement. This statement is what action you need to take to reach your vision. In sports terms, your vision is the big win. The mission statement is your game plan. They need to be in sync so that your actions match your ultimate goal. For example, the mission statement for my client's first vision statement is:

"I will achieve my vision by conducting regular visits to our retail outlets to meet customers. I will also establish an internal group to review and implement customer suggestions."

The mission statement for his second vision statement is:

"I will educate the human resources and financial industries by joining and participating in organizations such as the Human Resources Management Association of Chicago and Association of Financial Professionals. I will also write articles and a blog so I can inform and educate industry professionals. I will establish myself as THE expert."

Creating a vision and mission statement can seem like a daunting task, but the best way to overcome a block is to start writing. Trust yourself to recognize your vision and mission; you have more insight into your dreams than you might think.

—————— STRATEGY TO MARKET AND GROW YOUR BRAND

Developing your personal brand is the next step in taking back your career. Your personal brand is how you package yourself for the marketplace. Your brand dictates how others perceive you. Similar to a television commercial for a product, you want to elicit positive emotions from your audience. Your personal brand includes how you describe yourself, how others see you, what need you fill in the marketplace, and what makes you stand out.

From now on, you are the product, and your job is to sell yourself. There are three steps in the personal brand development process:

Who you are = Features

What makes you different = Benefits

What you contribute = Value

Your **features** include your experience, talents, education, goals, ethics, and accomplishments.

Your **benefits** are what you bring to the market because of your features. For example, one of your features may be that you have enough experience in your career field that you won't need to be trained. The benefit is that this will save a company money and time. Another feature may be your specific accomplishments. The benefit is that, because of your track record, you have proved that can deliver stellar results again and again.

Next we have **value**—or what you can contribute that sets you apart from the rest of the pack. A good way to figure that out is to list the top twenty accomplishments throughout your career and then ask yourself, *"So what?"* after each accomplishment.

Here's an example of an accomplishment: *Led team of six engineers in major software conversion project. The project affected two hundred and fifty clients and took three months to complete. We finished project two months earlier than scheduled.*

Okay—so what?

— We saved the company $30,000 by completing the project early
— We set a new project turnaround timeframe
— We documented the project process so that other departments could use it
— We didn't lose any clients during the conversion
— We proved we could successfully collaborate with other departments throughout the project

When you're asking, "So what?", you're really asking, "How did we measure our success?" For example, how much money did we save? How did we improve processes or training? What improvements did we make to customer service? What did we learn from the accomplishment? People want to know what difference you make and how effective you are. They want to know how you impact the success of an organization, so telling them about your past experiences is a great way to build credibility and help them visualize how you can help their business.

———————————————— **BRANDING YOURSELF NOW**

Writing a two-sentence introduction for yourself is a good way to start the branding process. Think about how you want people to perceive you when you initially meet them. What would be important to include in your two sentences? Obviously, your name is good, as is what industry you're in. Adding something of interest to the listener is helpful. For example:

> *"Hello, my name is Ben Drake, and I'm a sales executive in the soft-ware industry. I got laid off a few months ago, and I'm looking for a new challenge."*

Okay, so we know your name is Ben Drake, you're in the software industry, and you're looking for a new job. But how compelling is this introduction? How could you improve on it?

The first step is to write thirty-five words that describe you. Here are some to help you get started:

Articulate	Accomplished	Perceptive	Consistent
Accurate	Driven	Leader	Critical
Flexible	Manager	Loyal	Tenacious
Detail-Oriented	Diligent	Careful	Patient
Organized	Innovative	Unique	
Thoughtful	Team Player	Powerful	
Smart	Professional	Successful	

Once you've come up with your descriptors, prioritize the top five. You'll use these in your introduction. Make a hard copy of the other words and post them on your refrigerator, bathroom mirror, or some place where you will see them daily. These words will remind you of how talented and accomplished you are—and help you remember to use these words when you talk about yourself.

So, let's say that you, Ben, have chosen the following words as your top five: outgoing, knowledgeable, smart, professional, successful. You might amend your introduction to something like this:

"Hi. My name is Ben, and I'm one of a select few who knows how to position cloud computing in your organization to make you the industry leader."

You'll notice I didn't use every descriptor. However, I implied that Ben is smart, professional, and successful. Using an introduction like this leaves the door open for the listener to say, "Tell me more." This is the reaction you want. You now have the opportunity to ask questions about what the listener needs—questions such as, "What do you know about cloud computing?" or "What challenge would cloud computing help you address?" The idea is to develop your brand through a strategic, thoughtful—and, most importantly—two-sided dialogue.

———————————— CREATE A BUZZ ABOUT YOUR BRAND

Ten years ago, it was very difficult to create excitement about yourself. You would need to hire a public relations firm and spend a fair amount of cash. Today, you can promote yourself through free social networking sites like LinkedIn, Twitter, Facebook, and blogs. While you are getting information out about yourself through social networking, you will also be practicing your "story." Your story is a combination of your vision, mission, and brand, and each of us has one. Develop your story by writing a few sentences using a combination of your descriptors, plus a piece of information to help the listener understand more about you. For example:

> *"Hello, my name is John Wolfe, and I'm in the talent business. I'm a successful corporate recruiter who knows how to match quality candidates with outstanding companies. I can manage your hiring process to drastically increase your hiring success and grow your company."*

John's introduction and story gives the listener great information. The use of "talent business" piques the listener's interest so that he wants to hear more. The next sentence tells the listener John's feature, which is matching candidates to companies. The last sentence spells out John's benefit—growing the company and decreasing the chance of bad hires.

Your story is an integral part of creating a buzz about your brand. Here are a few steps to getting it just right:

— Write your story out and read it out loud. You may feel self-conscious at first, and that's very normal. This process will help you build your confidence.

— Test it in the marketplace. Practice on people that you trust. Choose three friends or colleagues, and ask them for feedback to questions like: Is my story believable? Is it interesting? Does it fit my image? Is it too long?

— Adjust your story according to feedback. Practice it again for a week, and then continue to refine it as you become more comfortable and confident in your delivery.

Understanding and delivering your story is integral to building a buzz about your brand—which you'll do through networking.

———— GAME PLAN TO NETWORK THE REST OF YOUR LIFE

I learned the hard way how important an active, effective network is. When I was laid off the first time, in 1990, I hadn't kept my network alive. Take it from me: There's nothing worse than a dead network. Trying to get your career back on track after a layoff is a major project, and rebuilding a network slowed me down considerably. I resolved that I would never be in that position again. Now I keep my network growing by calling contacts on a quarterly basis. I stay on the lookout for articles of interest and forward them to my network through LinkedIn. I try to be a resource to others, and it pays off because people remember me and will help me when I need it.

For instance, when I wanted an introduction into a local company but didn't have any connections, I decided to find a person in my network who knew someone in my target company. I made sure that I incorporated my request into every conversation I had. It took several weeks, but I accumulated the names and introductions I wanted. These connections didn't turn into business immediately, so I also learned about being patient and nurturing business relationships. Networking for the rest of your life means that you start connecting the dots every time you talk to someone. By that, I mean you start thinking about how *you* can help the person you're talking to, as well as how they can help you.

Todd, for example, is a connection of mine who was interested in changing jobs. He was an executive director at a non-profit, but he wanted more challenge. He asked me to help him connect with people who could expand his network. I was on the board of directors for a non-profit, so I was able to put him in touch with contacts who, in turn, gave him additional names. Todd eventually took a new director position at another non-profit that was just starting to interview for the position when he introduced himself. In the coming chapters, I'll discuss strategies and give step-by-step advice for building a healthy network and becoming a resource to others.

THE NEW CAREER GAME

What we've been talking about—determining your vision, mission, and brand—is essential to succeeding in what I call the new career game. The following diagram depicts the cycle of the new career game.

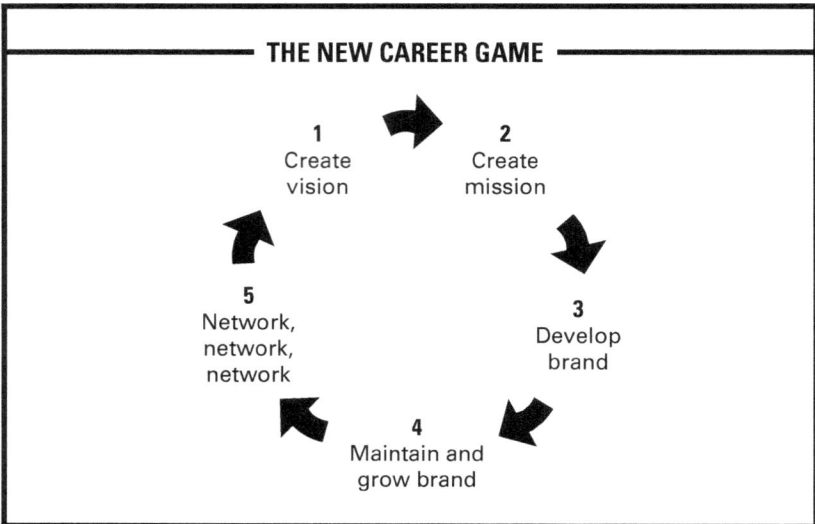

THE NEW CAREER GAME

1 Create vision

2 Create mission

3 Develop brand

4 Maintain and grow brand

5 Network, network, network

Let's look at an example of how to use this cycle in real life.

Bill, a recent client who was a marketing executive for an advertising agency, needed to restart his career. When he was laid off, he decided to go about his job search in a different way. He'd read about personal branding and how others were using social networking in their job search, and after attending a seminar I was giving, he asked me to help him define his job search campaign. Using the New Career Game diagram, Bill developed an outline to help him take charge of his life and career:

Bill's vision statement: "I will create a successful small start-up marketing company."

Bill's mission statement: "I will provide cost-effective online marketing solutions for midsized financial services organizations."

Bill's brand: I am a marketer who can produce major league marketing campaigns for clients and achieve winning results.

Maintain and grow brand: Bill built a website and launched a blog showcasing challenges his clients faced and solutions Bill's company created for them. He made it a point to become visible both online and in his community. First he joined LinkedIn and asked clients to write recommendations for him. Then he joined the local chambers of commerce and supported local businesses by participating in various community events.

Bill discovered that once he knew what he wanted and how to think and talk about himself as a brand (for example, he wanted his potential clients to know he had Fortune 500 experience and could give them top-shelf programs at reasonable pricing), it was much easier to solicit help from others. His network has doubled, and his contacts are high quality. He's much more confident, and his sales pipeline is full. Bill is in the running for a major contract with a Fortune 500 company.

As you can see from Bill's experience, developing your personal vision and mission statements provides a solid base for creating your brand.

In this chapter, you've started positioning yourself to reinvent your career by creating your vision and mission statements. These two guiding declarations are the first step in taking ownership of who you are and what you contribute to the market. Armed with your extensive product knowledge (remember, *you're* the product, so you know your features and benefits better than anyone), you have begun to develop a brand identity and marketing plan. With these tools, you will be able to shift your position on the field from defense to offense—and the next chapter will teach you how to develop a winning team that will help you cover all the bases.

CHAPTER FOUR

PICKING YOUR WINNING TEAM

" Talent wins games, but teamwork and intelligence win championships. " —MICHAEL JORDAN

WHY is it that we use teams for so many things in our lives? We have a financial team to manage our money and a medical team for our health care. Our kids are on soccer, football, baseball, basketball, or swim teams. Chances are, we work with a team of people for various projects at work or church. Yet, when it comes to managing our careers, we usually don't give much thought to picking a winning team.

I work with many clients who are going through a career transition without a team. They tell me how lonely and isolating the experience is—how they feel directionless and unfocused. They also feel very overwhelmed. Unless you are extremely disciplined, the lack of structure, ideas, and inspiration from others can sideline you in short order.

Early in my career, I was very lucky to have a mentor who helped me understand what a team approach looked like and how it can be successful. She encouraged me to surround myself with colleagues who were good at things I wasn't. In order to fill those blanks, I had to take time and be very honest with myself about what I was good at and where I needed help. To start, I made a list of activities I enjoyed doing and those I often procrastinated before starting. I realized that I excelled at developing the strategic planning process and implementing new ideas. I was very good at asking questions like, "What if we tried doing a project a different way?" What I *didn't* do well was routing tasks and detail work like completing expense forms or weekly project reports. I discovered that I wanted to introduce new ideas and technology to an organization, but I didn't want to maintain it. I also confirmed for myself that I am very extroverted and need to be around people. If I had to stay in an office all day, I wasn't as productive.

After going through this process, I was able to find colleagues who could help me strengthen those aspects of my job that were more challenging for me. I mentored them in return and always made sure they received credit for their assistance. Today, my company's details are handled by THE detail person... my husband, John! I also have a business career coach who keeps me accountable for the yearly goals she helps me set. Starting a business is exciting, but there are lots of details, and it can be a very solitary endeavor. My coach reminds me to finish the projects I start and encourages me to set the bar higher for myself.

You want all the advantages you can get in managing your career. Trying to conduct a job search or career analysis alone tends to extend the process. During one of my layoffs, I spent hours in front of the computer researching job websites. After a month of this, I found that I was getting lazier and becoming sullen. I wasn't getting any interaction. No one answered my emails. No one cared that I was looking for a job. No one knew I was in my basement madly sending out thousands of resumes. The real danger came when I caught myself sitting around in my workout clothes watching old black-and-white "Perry Mason" reruns. It was time to form my team, set goals, and get back on track.

Your career management team is your sounding board. They believe in you and want you to succeed, and they help you stay focused during your search by giving you information and different perspectives. Your team is crucial to your success and accountability.

Include the following disciplines on your team (which will change as your needs change):

— Finance
— Banking
— Recruitment
— Career coach
— Two colleagues in your industry

The finance and banking team members will help you ease what is usually the biggest source of stress. For instance, Alex needed help putting together an operating budget. He asked a former colleague, who was a financial services professional, to join his team. His colleague agreed and provided Alex with the guidance he needed to put together a sound budget. Another one of my clients asked his financial planner and a banker friend to join his team. He didn't know a recruiter, so he tapped into my network to meet one. Finding a recruiter can be challenging, but don't give up looking. Ask colleagues whom they have used, and work your social media connections—which we'll discuss more later—to get references.

Asking colleagues to help you with your transition can be a humbling experience—just remember that people want to help and will be open to your request if you are clear about what you want them to contribute.

So, what do you want from your team?

— Ideas on how to enlarge your network
— Support
— Accountability

IDEAS ON HOW TO ENLARGE YOUR NETWORK

Your team can help come up with several ideas about enlarging your business network. This principle is especially true for members on your team who work in different industries than you do; they will have contacts you probably won't have in your current network because they work with a completely different group of people. Your team may also have contacts through their churches, colleges, or professional associations.

SUPPORT

The support you want is belief in your abilities and open, honest conversations in which you can discuss your job-hunting strategy. There will be times when you feel as though you're not achieving any results. That's when your team can step in and point out where you might need to make adjustments. Your team gives you other points of view.

Mark had been a manager for ten years, and he was getting burned out in his present position. He was doing the job of three people because colleagues were laid off and not replaced. He worked long hours and felt as if he were never going to finish any of the fifteen projects he was involved in. The frustration was starting to affect his family as well. Mark knew he was going down fast—he needed help and support. Eventually, he decided to call on five people to help him sort things out. He chose two college friends, his former boss, his minister and his financial planner. Without realizing it, Mark had just formed his career management team. The team now meets once a quarter and helps Mark set priorities. They also recommended that he take a time management course and work with his supervisor on expectations. Just having a few people who are willing to listen and offer ideas can help you keep your sanity.

ACCOUNTABILITY

Holding you accountable is the biggest gift your team can give you. Being answerable to people you trust keeps you focused on the end goal.

Chuck was six months into his search for a controller position. He was attending three networking events a week but not meeting contacts who could help him. Chuck recalls always taking his "one sheet" (a shorter version on his resume) to the meetings, but he didn't have a strategy for whom he wanted to meet and what he would say. He left with a pocket full of business cards but no new *connections*.

Networking didn't come naturally to Chuck, and he hated every minute of it. He was diligent about going to three events a week because he had made that his goal, but he had very little to show for his efforts. When he brought this challenge up to his team, one member asked why he continued to attend networking groups if he wasn't getting the results he wanted. Chuck didn't have a good answer. The team suggested that he set criteria for what meetings he would attend in the future. Here's an example of what he put together:

Event/Date	Intro	Goal	First Approach Strategy
Executive Networking	Practice new introduction and see how it works	Meet two people in my industry	Look to see if I know anyone. If not, talk to someone who's standing alone.

Chuck used this template and explained that it helped him accomplish the following:

— remember why he was attending an event
— meet people in his industry
— meet people out of his industry
— meet the speaker at the event
— practice his introduction
— set a goal for attending the event
— meet ten new people and decide what category they fell into
— determine how much time he would spend talking to a person

Chuck's team helped him find an approach that redefined the concept of networking for him.

HOW TO CHOOSE THE BEST PLAYERS

Decide the criteria you want to use for your teammates. Start with a small group; you can always enlarge it if you need to. Consider what issues you face and what kinds of experienced people you need. Choose people you trust and who have talents that complement yours. And don't limit yourself to colleagues in your industry; asking someone from another discipline will give you a different point of view, helping you see your challenges from all angles. You want to consider all your options and surround yourself with people who can help you uncover all pros and cons. Include people who have strong networks and are willing to introduce you to them.

TEAM MEETINGS

Because you're the captain of this team, you want to be prepared with an agenda for each meeting and keep your sessions to a reasonable amount of time—sixty minutes or less. You'll want to be very clear with each team member about what you expect and want from him or her. Remember, their time is valuable, so make sure each meeting is productive. Here's a sample team meeting agenda:

ACCOUNTABILITY TEAM MEETING

Review your marketing plan	10 min.
Updates on action items	10 min.
Discussions on upcoming interview	10 min.
Target company review	10 min.
Feedback	15 min.

You can begin your meeting by updating your team about what you've done since the last meeting to reach goals that you've set. You want to set the tone of your meetings by letting them know what you've accomplished. Your action items may include attending networking events, responding to position postings, and research on companies you've identified as organizations you want to work for. If you have an interview coming up soon, you'll want to get interviewing tips from your team. The team can also practice interviewing techniques like panel interviews and phone interviews. It's a good idea to review the companies you're researching and have targeted to network into. Finally, asking for feedback about your progress, marketing plan, branding, and any other topics that come up is essential so that you're not working in a vacuum.

STAYING IN TOUCH WITH YOUR TEAM

Once you've selected and formed your team, it's essential that you maintain regular communication. My client, John, selects one of his top team members to contact every six weeks. He makes an appointment on his calendar to take his team member to coffee or just have a short phone conversation. During that time, he catches the team member up on his progress but *also* listens to him or her to find out if there's an opportunity to offer his expertise. The result? In addition to regular support, his team now calls him to tell him about open positions and industry updates.

I can't emphasize enough how important your team is to you. Keeping your perspective and staying in a positive space is very difficult to do by yourself. Let your team help you. And remember to thank them regularly. Let them know you'll be there when they need you. We all need each other, and we're stronger when we team with other smart people!

Now that you see the importance of choosing a dynamic team, it's time to start getting into playing shape. Every athlete will tell you that you won't be effective if you're out of shape. The next chapter is going to give you a great workout!

CHAPTER FIVE

GETTING INTO PLAYING SHAPE

" Even if you are on the right track, you'll get run over if you just sit there. " —WILL ROGERS

TODAY'S career game is like any other contact sport: Getting in playing shape is critical to success.

Being in playing shape includes the body and mind. When people are stressed out because of a career transition, they often neglect to take care of themselves. That neglect can take the form of overeating, undereating, drinking too much, not getting enough sleep, or one of many other unhealthy habits. Pay attention to how you react to major stress so you know what you need to watch out for. For example, I've learned that I skip meals and don't exercise when tension is high. I also know that my mental state reflects when I'm not in shape physically. I begin to be very critical of my body and feel exhausted and down all the time. Because I don't eat, my energy level is low, so my attitude isn't positive. My self-esteem is diminished, and I'm not fun or inspirational to be around; who wants to hire someone in that condition? On the other hand, when you eat correctly, exercise regularly, and get enough sleep, you'll look and feel great. You want to be at your very best during a transition.

Your mental conditioning is just as important as your physical conditioning. All successful players will tell you that mental training in conjunction with getting their bodies into playing shape determines their success.

Let's take a more detailed look at what attributes you need to be in playing shape:

STAMINA

Stamina is the capability of sustaining a prolonged stressful effort. Every great athlete has loads of it, and so do you; you just may not be giving yourself credit for it.

One of my clients, Chuck, exemplifies this ability to "hang in there" when the situation is challenging. Chuck is an IT executive who was recently in a career transition. A marathon runner, Chuck runs five miles every weekday and seventeen miles on the weekends in preparation for his races. He also visualizes how he will cross the finish line. When he was in career transition, he added a new exercise to his routine: visualizing his new position and with whom he would be working. This technique was especially valuable during the temporary job he took for a large consumer goods organization. There, he was one of fifty IT temps who wrote very complicated code in a crowded room with no cubicles. A common joke among the temps was, "Don't leave your chair unoccupied for more than ten minutes because someone will take it." Several languages were spoken during the day, and conference calls were conducted in small groups all over the room with no soundproofing. Hanging over his head the whole time was the knowledge that his contract could end at any time.

To make it through (and continue to pay the bills while proceeding with his job search), Chuck had to learn how to shut out all the distractions and accomplish his coding. He learned to be flexible and stay positive. These qualities paid off, because even though he was at a job with no security and no future, recruiters were more willing to talk to him because he was working. He landed five interviews and eventually accepted an offer with a large international bank. The position was newly created and exactly matched his expertise. He got the salary and benefits package he wanted. Chuck noted that staying in marathon shape—both physically and mentally—gave him confidence and a belief in himself that carried him through a very rough two years.

Take a few moments to assess times when you've displayed your stamina. What were those situations and how did you perform? How did pacing yourself help you then, and how will it help you now? To increase your stamina, prioritize your work and practice time management. When you feel overwhelmed, reduce stress by taking a deep breath. Then quickly assess what you need to do, prioritize, and set realistic completion timeframes. Ask for help when you need to.

CONFIDENCE

Geena was a financial planner. She came to me because she was ready to make a career move but didn't know where to start. Because she hadn't done career planning in many years, she wanted to sharpen herself both physically and mentally. One of Geena's biggest challenges was the "peanut gallery" in her head. You know what I'm talking about— your peanut gallery talks to you all day long. The messages can be positive or negative, depending on how you've programmed yourself. And sometimes your peanut gallery doesn't get the new memo you sent about a message you want to give yourself. The messages from your peanut gallery might sound something like this:

"Wait till they find out how stupid you really are. Then they'll finally know the truth!"

"You need to get a few more pieces of information, and then you'll be really ready."

"You'll never be good enough or smart enough."

"You're too old."

"You're too young."

"You'll never make it in the big leagues."

These messages showed up for Geena when she was undergoing change or feeling increased pressure. I helped her reprogram her self-messages, because most of the information was false. It didn't happen overnight, but after practice and commitment, Geena learned to give herself powerful motivating messages.

Don't underestimate the effect that positive self-talk will have on your confidence, especially during a challenging time. Pam is a human resource professional who specializes in labor relations and performance management. She is in a career transition, and I asked her how she keeps her confidence up. Her answer was telling.

"I use positive affirmations and self-talk," she said. "I volunteer to help others. I have daily contact with others. When I get down, I review my accomplishments; I identify the situation as I found it, the action I took, and, most importantly, the results I achieved. This exercise reminds me of my skills and successes. I also review my LinkedIn recommendations regularly. When I need some reassurance, I ask for it."

What kind of messages do you give yourself? Record any negative messages using this table. Create a new message to replace the message holding you back. For example:

Old Message	New Message
I'm not smart enough.	I'm very smart. I work hard. I'm proud of my accomplishments.
I'm not prepared enough.	I'm thoroughly prepared and I know what I'm presenting. I know more than my audience about this subject.

COMMITMENT

Dana is a marketing and IT executive who felt stymied because there was no excitement in her job. She decided she would stay where she was while looking for a new position.

However, when she started an inventory of what she needed to do to begin her search, she realized that she wasn't confident about her image... particularly her weight. She had given herself six months to find a new job. But instead of jumping into revising her resume or calling a search firm, she started an exercise program where she worked out an hour a day. Within a month, Dana felt better about herself because she'd lost eight pounds. In addition, the physical activity was affecting her mental attitude because she felt a sense of accomplishment. Dana actually looked forward to her workouts. She was learning that staying with the exercise program helped her stay focused, sleep better, and feel better about herself and what she could accomplish.

What Dana didn't know when she started her job search was that she would need to be strong and committed. She had found out about a great available position through a friend, who put her in contact with the human resources vice president. Dana's first interview was a phone interview that went well, so the next step was a face-to-face panel interview. The panel interview was a success, and another interview was scheduled with two other department heads.

Here's where Dana's endurance came into play: She had *eleven* interviews with the same company over the next two months, including several one-to-one interviews with senior leaders, panel sessions with every department she would work with, and phone interviews with potential international coworkers. The long interview process was a screening device. If a candidate made it through, it showed that he or she had met one of the company's major criteria for their employees: commitment.

The company eventually made Dana an offer that she accepted. She has been at her new job for a year. She also continued her exercise routine and ran in her first marathon. Dana made a commitment to get into and stay in top physical form, and she says that commitment changed her life. She feels more powerful than ever.

GETTING INTO PLAYING SHAPE

Winners practice being successful. Winners have a vision for their lives. Winners know that what they focus on becomes reality. When you think about being a failure, your energy level goes down and you lose your winning edge.

This is how one of my clients, John, explained how he approached getting into shape: "You don't just get out of bed one morning and decide to play football when you haven't touched a football since you were in the eighth grade!" he said. "Exercising, pacing yourself, and practicing are the first steps."

John was an IT executive who worked for an insurance company. He knew there was little room for him to move up; his company had been merged with another company two years earlier and promotions had virtually disappeared. Because of this, John chose to look for another position in the insurance industry.

Knowing he would need a structured "workout routine," John developed the following project plan to capture the key activities and dates in his job search:

Vision Statement: I will be an innovative and purposeful professional who leads by example.

Mission Statement: I will work for an organization that demonstrates its commitment to clients and employees. I will make significant contributions to every facet of my career.

Marketing Activities	Details	Completion Date
Begin exercise program	60 minutes/three times/week	Ongoing
Reinforce self-confidence	Reinforce self-confidence by reminding myself of major accomplishments	Ongoing
Develop list of target companies	20 companies I'm interested in working for	Two months from today

Marketing Activities	Details	Completion Date
Research target companies	Research on Internet and conduct informational interviews	Three months from today
Create personal brand	Begin using social media: Facebook, LinkedIn, Twitter	One month from today
Complete accreditation program	Pass online programs	Two months from today

John understood the importance of practice in getting into playing shape. His dedication led to winning the new position he wanted. He reclaimed control of his career by *consciously preparing* himself to move forward.

ELIMINATE VISITS TO "PITY CITY"

I once had a manager who told clients, "You can visit Pity City, but you can't live there!" We all experience rough times in our careers, and when we do, it's easy to slip into the pity mode and spread our negativity to everyone around us.

So how do you get into playing shape when faced with negative attitudes? First and foremost, set boundaries for yourself. When you run into a negative mine field, recognize it and put your shields up. Don't get lured into the conversation. Remember that you're in training to get into the best playing shape you can. You deserve to take care of yourself and put YOU first.

Here are two exercises to keep you out of Pity City.

Take an afternoon and go somewhere quiet. Write down all the things you don't want to do in your next job (i.e., boring work, working with stupid people, etc.). Write as many items as you can think of in thirty minutes. Once you've completed this exercise, look at each entry carefully and prioritize your top ten. This will help you see what you really don't want in your next position and will also help you eliminate feelings about the things you don't want in your career. Once you've written down the gripes, you feel lighter.

Now take thirty minutes and write down all the things you do want in your next job. Think about every possible situation and person who can make this job perfect. Notice how you feel while you're completing this exercise. Writing about positive situations and the way you want your workplace to be gives you more energy and helps you become more positive.

Pity City drags you down. The less time you spend there the better.

GAUGE YOUR FITNESS LEVEL

What kind of playing shape are you in? Here are some questions to help you determine your current level of fitness.

1   Have you created your personal brand?
  a   Develop an image of how you want to be perceived in the marketplace. Decide what you want to be known for.
  b   Create a differentiating statement (i.e., "I'm not just a sales executive. I'm a sales executive who increased sales by forty percent in my last position," or "I'm not just a communications professional. I'm a communications professional who is recognized for an award-winning employee information campaign.")

2   How are you building your online presence?
  a   What social networking media are you using? Facebook, LinkedIn, Twitter?
  b   Consider writing a blog as a daily or weekly written communication tool. Some examples are: www.highgainco.blogspot.com, www.zenhabits.com, www.mashable.com, and www.openforum.com/connectodex/how-to-change-the-world.

3   How do you measure how effective your network is?
  a   Develop criteria for an "A" category contact. An "A" category contact is a person who readily shares other contact names

with you. People in this category truly understand how to network and will help you make contacts by personally introducing you to their network. "A" category contacts always follow through and do what they promise. They're usually in your profession and know the movers and shakers.

4 What professional associations or networking groups do you belong to?

a Associations and networking groups give you professional exposure to your industry. As you become more involved in these groups, you can be a resource for others by becoming a subject matter expert. This will give you credibility and also help you build your industry networking.

5 When did you last upgrade your skills? What options are available to you?

a Look into continuing education courses offered through professional associations. There are also many online courses and seminars you can take. Attending workshops and seminars in person also gives you the opportunity to network and meet new people.

6 What are the current trends in your industry?

a Are there any mergers, international competition, or new technologies you should be aware of? How do they affect you?

7 Have you published any informational articles using your expertise?

a What topic(s) could you write about?

b Who is your target audience?

c Where could you get your article published?

8 How current is your headshot (professional picture of you)?

a Does your photo fit your personal branding image?

b When can you update it?

9 How current is your professional bio?

    a Your bio is a one-page document that gives a snapshot of your career and accomplishments. Update your bio at least once a year.

10 What books are you reading?

    a Being well-read is a plus in today's market because it shows that you have a life outside the office. You'd be surprised how many people talk about the latest book they're reading. It's a safe topic to bring up at any social event, and reading makes you more interesting and well rounded.

How did you do? These questions are meant to help you gauge what it takes to get into shape. Your goal is to get yourself in a position to answer all of these questions confidently and positively. You should return to this questionnaire at least once a year to check up on your playing shape.

Doesn't it feel great getting into shape and beginning to create your game plans? It's important work that will pay off for you very soon. Now it's all about taking what you've learned so far and implementing your plan. The next chapter will help you do just that.

CHAPTER SIX

YOUR GAME-WINNING PLAYS

" The spirit, the will to win, and the will to excel are the things that endure. These qualities are so much more important than the events that occur. " —VINCE LOMBARDI

THIS is probably the most important chapter in this playbook because here's where we get down to the "nitty gritty" plan and execution of your winning plays. In this chapter, you will create a working marketing plan—a game plan to guide you to playing your best every day. Without it, you could wander the playing field for months and get nothing accomplished. The plan is also a tool for goal setting, progress measurement, and accountability. Let's review the elements of your plan and get to work!

MARKETING PLAN

Your marketing plan is a concise, easy-to-read document that you develop to use on a daily basis. Your plan should be the first thing you read in the morning; set your day up by reminding yourself about your vision and mission and reviewing your goals. Your plan includes the following:

— Your vision and mission statements
— Product definition
— Target market information
— Marketing materials overview

VISION AND MISSION STATEMENTS

Your vision and mission statements are critical to developing the foundation for your career and life. Creating a powerful vision of what you want to accomplish in your career and how you plan to accomplish it prepares you for action. When you take time to write out your vision and mission, you take ownership of your dreams. Writing it takes you from ideas to concrete actions. The cover page of your marketing plan will consist of the phrase "Marketing Plan for [Your Name]" and the current date centered on the middle of the page. The next page is your vision and mission statements.

PRODUCT DEFINITION

Whether you realize it or not, you are (and will continue to be) a sales and marketing person. I'll say it again: **You are the product.** You are always selling yourself.

Selling yourself can be easy, or it can be the hardest thing you ever do. It's up to you. As I mentioned in an earlier chapter, we are taught to not talk about ourselves and how talented we are. Clients tell me often about how hard it is to talk about themselves. They know they're missing out on great opportunities to let others know what value they bring to the market; however, the nagging word that creeps into their minds is "bragging." Let me give you the lowdown on this whole bragging notion. Chances are that somewhere along the line, parents or teachers drilled into your head that bragging about yourself was bad. It was showing off, and parents or teachers would quickly put you in your place. (If you were raised in the Midwest, you know exactly what I'm talking about.) But at this point in your career and life, it's time to put "bragging" in a new context. Start thinking of it as *marketing*.

Ask yourself, "What do I bring to the market? What is my value to a company? How can I impact the bottom line? What results have I delivered?" Develop your marketing pitch based on the answers to these questions.

Paul is a successful sales manager. One of his biggest challenges is to talk about his accomplishments and why he's been a top producer. Paul says that he can sell any product or service his company has, but when it comes to selling himself, he has real problems. He sells himself short and says things like, "Anyone can motivate a sales team," or, "Anyone can make cold calls." What Paul fails to realize is that not just "anyone" can do it successfully and consistently like he does!

One very effective way to overcome the bragging syndrome is to use a three-step process. Write down your ten biggest career accomplishments. First, briefly (in two sentences) describe the situation or problem you were working on. Second, (again in two or three sentences) describe what action you took to address the problem. Third, and most importantly, list the results of the action you took. Here's an example:

Situation: Our company was introducing a new service, but there was no plan for how the service would be introduced in the market.

Action: I developed a marketing introduction plan that included sales goals, identified the target audience, set a budget, suggested internal and external resources, and set timeframes.

Results: This was the most successful new product launch in the company's history. Sales goals were exceeded by forty percent. Market share increased twelve percent. The service is now the industry standard.

As you work on this exercise, also remember your features and benefits we discussed in Chapter 3. Think about products that you buy. You buy a certain brand of computer because of price, size, weight, and power. These are features of the product. You also buy the computer because it was recommended by someone you trust or because you've had a good experience with the product. In addition, you buy this brand of computer for the benefits you get from it (saving money or time, increased efficiencies, etc.).

Using this example, return to thinking about *your* features (i.e., education, training, experience, accomplishments, talents). Now add benefits to those features. Consider a statement such as, "I could save the company money because I can hit the ground running." Or, "I could save the company time because I've been through many conversions and I understand how to put plans in place; the last conversion I was responsible for saved the company $2,000,000." It's very important that you state your feature followed by a benefit. Here's another example: "Because I'm detail-oriented, I make sure there aren't any surprises for management." Here, you're explaining what your feature is (detail-oriented) followed by the benefits (no surprises). Here's another one: "I'm very process-oriented, which means I dependable, follow the rules, and get the job done quickly."

Okay, now let's put it all together: situation, action, results, features, and benefits: "When I was hired as the human resource manager, there were no written job descriptions. I am very goal-oriented so I wanted to develop the job descriptions and get them approved and instituted by management by the end of the next quarter. I met that deadline. Having jobs descriptions enabled both managers and employees to measure their effectiveness and results."

Now, let's dissect this story. The situation was that there were no written job descriptions. Your feature is that you are goal-oriented and results-driven, so you got the descriptions written, approved, and used by the end of the quarter. The benefits are that the company now has a way to measure performance. All together, this is a strategic way of marketing yourself—*not* bragging! This will be the second page of your marketing plan.

──────────────── TARGET MARKET INFORMATION

Your target market is the group you're marketing to—the people or companies who need you. Your mission and vision define your target market. If your vision is to have a major impact on people's lives and your mission is to be a CEO, your target audience is a company looking for a CEO (or perhaps your present organization). Define this group in as much detail as possible so your message is specific.

Your target market has three legs:

— **Existing industry:** where your career has been
— **New industry:** where your career could flourish
— **Your dream industry:** the wild card "if I could do anything I wanted" career

Decide which market you want to focus on, and sell yourself to that group using the achievements, features, and benefits you came up with for page two of your marketing plan.

The easiest group to attack first is the market in which you currently work, because it is the one you know the most about. Your major contacts are in this demographic. You are a known entity with people, and you understand their needs. The audience speaks the same jargon and is open to hearing about you. For all these reasons, this market is a great place to try out different marketing approaches to discover what works best. Look at this audience as the audition group.

For example, Joe is in the produce and perishable goods industry. He was a senior executive who brokered with suppliers for a large grocery chain. Joe knows that some of his company's recent business decisions have put his job in jeopardy. Fortunately, Joe is well known in his industry, and he decided to brand himself in the marketplace through the National Produce Association. He became a board member of the group and contributed to its newsletter and blog. He also began mentoring new professionals in his industry. Eventually, Joe became known as the "go to" guy in his field.

His next target was to expand his presence to complementary industries, so he chose wholesale florists. His goal was to become known and extend his brand. Joe understood that by enlarging his network into another industry, he would hear about career opportunities that might not be available to him otherwise. He made contacts in that industry through his existing network, and though he doesn't spend as much time on this focus, he's aware of who the movers and shakers are, and his name is familiar to them.

Joe's last marketing frontier is an area that has always intrigued him: organic farming. He only spends ten percent of his time researching organic farming because he knows he needs to focus mainly on working his current and complementary industries, but it's an area that could prove lucrative and fulfilling in the future.

Here's another example of how using target market information works. Beth has eleven years of sales experience in the financial services industry. However, she wanted to move into human resources—specifically, organizational development and training—so she focused her search on companies that sold training programs to corporations. She had several senior contacts from her previous sales positions, but her biggest challenge was to convince the target companies that her previous sales experience and success would translate to the sales of their product.

Beth knew this was a "relationship" sell. She leveraged her contacts to get introductions and formed relationships with decision-makers in the human resources departments. She also joined HR groups on LinkedIn and contributed to discussion topics to increase her visibility. It paid off, as Beth was soon invited to attend association meetings and meet people in the training sales arena. She focused fifty percent of her time on this strategy and the remaining time to answering job listings and interviewing. Her plan was to stay with this strategy for sixty days and see what inroads she could make in the sales training area. Because her relationships with previous clients had remained strong, Beth landed a new position in sales of corporate training programs fifty days into her search.

For a career transition, the areas of concentration are the same, with this twist:

— Current open positions
— Hidden jobs

Your target market includes (1) companies that have posted jobs and (2) companies that don't have publicly posted positions but that fit your criteria as organizations where you want to work. Keep your criteria level high but reasonable. Remember, these are organizations that may not have job listings right now. That's okay. They are on your list of companies to research and find out about their hidden job market. Some things to consider are company growth potential, company earnings, driving distance, industry, corporate culture, size of company, community involvement of organization, management style, public or privately held, and market share.

Zoe currently has a position with a large consumer goods corporation. However, she always has a Plan B, meaning that she keeps her resume updated and stays in touch with recruiters. Her Plan B is to seek out hidden jobs. She wants to keep herself marketable and network her way into two organizations that meet her "next job" criteria. The criteria include forward-thinking corporate culture, innovative product line, and room for advancement. Zoe knows that there may not be any positions open that she would apply for right now, but there may be openings in the future—and when that happens, hers will be a name already familiar to these companies.

We can become very complacent in our job search, both when we're "safely" in a position or looking for a new one. Understanding and continuing to educate your target market about yourself is a play that will give you an instant advantage in the field because most people stop networking and marketing themselves when they move into a new job. You don't disappear from the market when you get a new job or assignment. You stay out front with your personal marketing updates. You never want associates to say, "Whatever happened to what's her name?" Keeping your name in the marketplace is an ongoing activity that you will do for the rest of your career.

In your marketing plan, target market information is the third page.

Your marketing materials reflect your personal brand and tell your story. If you're creative and have a gift for writing and presenting information in a compelling way, take a day or two and create your own materials. If you're not creative and/or don't have funds to hire someone, I recommend you follow the "KISS" rule and keep it simple. Here's what you need:

— Professional headshot
— Updated generic resume
— One-page biography
— Business cards
— Two-sentence introduction
— LinkedIn profile
— Website
— Blog

Professional headshot: This is a photograph from the shoulders up that is taken by a professional photographer. It's a great investment because you can use it for online marketing such as LinkedIn, Facebook, your website and blog, and PowerPoint presentations.

Updated generic resume: Your updated generic resume is a document you keep and use when you're not actively in a job transition and you get a call from a recruiter or contact about a job opening. You can easily customize it by using the descriptions and requirements from the job posting. And remember—your resume is a marketing piece, so include your measurable accomplishments. Try to keep the length to two or three pages and use Arial font. *Always* have an updated resume. You never know when you'll need it!

One-page biography: This piece includes your headshot, contact information, and list of accomplishments. Here's an example of my bio. Notice that I hit the high points of my services and list several ways to contact me.

YOUR GAME-WINNING PLAYS

JAN MARINO BIO

Jan is a career management and personal branding expert, speaker, author, and founder of High Gain Companies, Inc. She is committed to helping clients develop a powerful personal brand and increase their business success. Today's career game is the ultimate contact sport, and the playing field, rules, teams, and plays have changed dramatically. Jan has been downsized, rightsized, oversized, and undersized, and she knows first-hand how career transitions can affect your life. Jan has worked with hundreds of clients, guiding them to taking back their personal power and moving forward with their lives. Her latest book, *Take Back Your Career,* was published in July 2011.

Jan can be reached at 630-299.9927, *jan.highgainco@gmail.com,* or check her out at www.linkedin.com/in/janmarino and www. highgaincompanies.com.

Business cards: Yes, you want business cards. They're an important tool in the career game because they're a "leave behind" with your contact information. Keep your business card design simple. Include your name, phone number, email address, and LinkedIn information. Use black or dark blue ink and Arial font. Under your name, use a couple of descriptors to let people know what industry and position you want (i.e., Human Resource Professional, Manufacturing or IT Professional, Health Services).

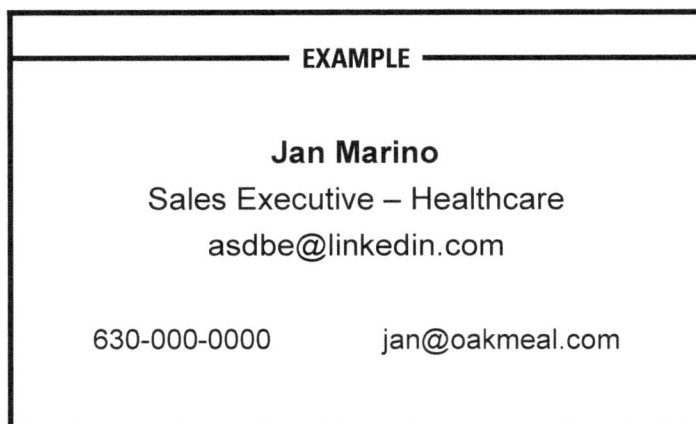

```
┌─────────────── EXAMPLE ───────────────┐
│                                        │
│              Jan Marino                │
│       Sales Executive – Healthcare     │
│          asdbe@linkedin.com            │
│                                        │
│   630-000-0000        jan@oakmeal.com  │
│                                        │
└────────────────────────────────────────┘
```

Two-sentence introduction: This short statement is the most important piece of marketing you have, so practice it until it becomes second nature to you. Rehearse in front of a mirror and watch your body language when you deliver your introduction. People make judgments on that first impression, and those judgments stay with them for a long time. I introduce myself with the following statements:

> *"Hi, I'm Jan Marino, and I'm a career management and personal branding expert. I've been downsized, rightsized, oversized, and undersized, so I understand careers and branding first hand."*

Try coming up with an introduction that is memorable and distinctive. You want to set yourself apart from the competition.

LinkedIn profile: In the new career game, your LinkedIn profile is your trading card. Your career statistics and accomplishments are visible here, and companies and search firms use LinkedIn to find candidates—it is a very powerful tool that helps build your personal brand and spread your marketing message!

Keep your LinkedIn profile short and inviting to read. Give the reader a reason to read, so write about your benefits. Don't copy and paste your resume! Here is an excellent example of an attention-getting, very readable profile. Note the use of keywords, such as "marketing executive," "new opportunities," and "strategy development"—which search engines will identify—and a promise to respond personally.

David is a results-oriented, hands-on marketing executive who identifies new opportunities, organizes the necessary team components, and spearheads strategy development to drive new avenues of revenue. Connect with me on LinkedIn using *partaind@mac.com*. When YOU connect with me, I will respond personally and am happy to review new technology solutions/ideas. I love connecting with marketing professionals with questions, observations, and business model discussions.

SPECIALTIES
- End-to-end project management
- Key Account management
- PC & Mac
- Strong financial background
- Product Marketing including product launch and strategic messaging
- Field sales support materials (presentations & brochures)
- Trade show & event organization
- Excellent written and communication skills
- B2B background

Website: In the new career game, a website is your opportunity to market your achievements and expertise to your target market—even before an interview. If you're unable to hire a professional website designer, there are a number of sites that allow you to build your own website through a free or low-cost template. However, this is one instance where "You get what you pay for" usually holds true, so keep the design simple if you go this route; a simple, well-edited website looks more professional than an attempt to get fancy with templates. Key thing to include on your website: your updated resume, a portfolio with links to past projects (if applicable), your one-page bio, your headshot, and your vision and mission statements. The goal is to make it easy for your target market to discern and buy into your brand.

Blog: If you have a particular expertise (and you do!) and are comfortable with your writing abilities, a blog is a fantastic tool for developing your online presence. A blog is dynamic—you can interact with others within and outside your field by referencing and linking to their blogs or articles, and you can share your knowledge directly with those who can use it. For your target market, it goes beyond a business card and website to give a snapshot glimpse into your personality and experience. Keep your blog active by posting two to three two-hundred word posts per week. Maintain visual interest by including a relevant graphic (photo, diagram, etc.) with each post, and engage your readers by asking questions. If you're not a "words person," consider starting a video blog (or vlog). The same principles apply, but you're addressing your audience directly with your face and voice—powerful tools! The keys to being a successful blogger or vlogger are simple: knowledge and confidence. And don't underestimate the power of proofreading!

When you're done creating and assembling your marketing materials, organize them into your Marketing Plan Worksheet. The following format is easy to complete, read, and update, and I recommend you keep this file online with your headshot, bio, business card format, and any other articles you will use in your job search.

MARKETING PLAN WORKSHEET – SAMPLE

Vision statement: I guide people to a secure retirement.

Mission statement: I will become an independently wealthy financial expert and resource for clients who want to retire successfully.

Branding statement: I am a certified and accredited financial planner who is experienced, honest, and loyal.

Product definition:
   Features: extensive knowledge of finances and investments, detail-oriented, honest, sensible, results-driven, down-to-earth, builds lasting relationships.

   Benefits: No panic, no surprises, keeps clients updated, saves clients time and money.

Target Audience: Goldman Sachs, Morgan Stanley, Citicorp, J.P. Morgan, Edward Jones, Raymond James, Merrill Lynch.

Marketing materials: Updated headshot, business card, resume, one-page biography, Linkedin, website, blog.

ONE MORE THING...

This marketing plan puts you in position to make game-winning plays— but it will do you no good if you're not *recording* those plays and their results. Think about it: Athletes learn how to improve by watching their past performances. They observe their actions and analyze why they did or didn't lead to a win. The same is true here. The last page of your marketing plan is one you should update every sixty days. It should contain two columns: The first is a detailed list of *all recent marketing activities* (e.g., which networking events you attended, how many blog posts you wrote, how many new contacts you added to LinkedIn, how many interviews you had, etc.); the second column should detail the results of those activities. Chances are, the longer you keep this record, the more patterns you'll see emerging—and, like professional athletes, you'll be able to determine which plays are working for you and which you can either improve upon or cut from your arsenal altogether. Ready to start making your plays? The next chapter will give you six scrimmages to start with.

CHAPTER SEVEN

SCRIMMAGES

❝ 100% of the shots you don't take don't go in. ❞ —WAYNE GRETZKY

EVERY athlete knows that regularly practicing plays leads to winning streaks. Coaches keep hundreds of plays under heavy secrecy so the opposition doesn't have an advantage. Scrimmages, or informal games between two segments of the same team, are off-limits to everyone but the most trusted personnel. Your best plays are designed by you and customized for your career game and plan. Rather than having hundreds of plays, I recommend you begin with just six. Trying to perfect more than six will frustrate you and set you up for failure. After you've got these six under your belt, you can add your own specially designed plays. Schedule yourself a reasonable amount of scrimmage time (two weeks to thirty days) to practice and measure your success.

In career management, scrimmages are practice sessions with your team and other trusted connections. In one way or another, the six scrimmages you're going to master involve how you introduce and talk about yourself. The old saying "practice makes perfect" is especially true when it comes to introducing yourself. You want your introduction to be natural and flow well, and you want to give just enough information so the listener is interested and wants to know more. **Start practicing with people you know… but not necessarily family.** Your family loves you. They know all your shortcomings as well as your strong points, which means they have a hard time being objective. They could be your worst critic or let you off the hook altogether. Instead, practice with your team every chance you get. Be open to feedback. Your team wants to help you become a better interviewer and networker, so take their feedback seriously. Ask someone to video your introduction so you can see yourself in action. Notice your body language and posture. Does it match your message? Are you confident? You will feel strange at first, and that's natural. Keep practicing until your introduction is second nature to you.

1. NETWORKING PLAY

My friend Terry likes to tell the story of her first networking experience. She heard about the event at work and thought it would be a good chance to meet people. Terry showed up ready to network but was overwhelmed when she walked into a room full of strangers. No one came up and talked to her, and she wasn't successful starting conversations with others. She decided to head for the bar and have a glass of wine… and you can probably guess the rest of the story. Terry got drunk and ended up with lots of business cards—from people she doesn't remember.

For some lucky people, networking comes easily and naturally. However, most of us are like Terry: We need lots of practice. Because you're going to be continuously building your network, practicing your networking skills will help ensure success. Practice also helps you become more comfortable with your introduction and conversational abilities. Your confidence is increased, and you become more relaxed with the networking process.

To start, find someone you know who's really good at networking and "shadow" him at a couple of events. This method works very well because it takes the pressure off so you can learn. While you're shadowing him, pay attention to his techniques: How does he approach a conversation? Listen carefully to the introduction and the small talk that follows. The person you are shadowing will introduce you, and this is your chance to practice the two-sentence introduction you developed in previous chapters. If you feel that twinge in your stomach, know two things—it's normal, and it never completely goes away. Believe it or not, that's a good thing. A little apprehension keeps you on your toes, and practice will help you use it to your best advantage.

The trick to successful networking, particularly at events, is to create a strategy before you go. Ask yourself these questions to put together your plan of attack.

What is your goal for attending the event? Set a goal to meet two new contacts who are in your industry. Set a further goal to add them to your LinkedIn connections. Find out as much about them as you can—what you have in common and how you can be of assistance to them. I met my client Walt at a networking event. This was the group's first meeting, but I knew just about everyone there. We were sitting down to listen to a presentation when a flustered guy appeared in the middle of the room. He looked lost, so I asked him to sit at our table. He told us that he had decided to walk to the event, and the walk had taken longer than he had anticipated. He was hot and sweaty, and his plans for a great networking adventure were quickly evaporating. He had been practicing his elevator speech and had planned to try it out at this event. His goal was to be calm and collected while introducing himself. Instead, he was out of breath and needed to cool down. The facilitator of the group had each table function independently and do a few exercises. Each person gave a short introduction and recalled one of his or her greatest accomplishments. Walt remembered his goal, took a deep breath, and introduced himself. He also used an example of how he had saved his former company several thousand dollars by improving the accounts receivable process. Although he told me afterwards he was shaking from fear, setting and remembering his goal for the meeting helped him salvage the situation—and make meaningful connections.

Whom will you talk to first? Start answering this question before even walking into a networking event. Begin by choosing your events carefully, finding out as much as you can about who will be attending. This will help you make the best use of your time, while also giving you a jump on conversation starters. At the event itself, don't count on someone talking to you first. If you don't know anyone, decide whom you'll walk up and introduce yourself to. I usually survey the room and look for someone who's alone, because it's harder to break into a group already in conversation. However, if there is no one alone, it's perfectly okay to join a conversation already in progress. Listen carefully the to topic, and if you have something to add to the conversation, introduce yourself—name only—and then make your contribution to the conversation. My mom gave me a great piece of advice that I remember when I go to events: Chances are you'll never see most of these people again, so what's the worst that can happen? In my experience, the worst that can happen is that you didn't try. Everyone at a networking event feels uncomfortable. Make things easier for *them* (and, thus, yourself) by being approachable and making eye contact. Smile and nod, inviting conversation. As you attend more events, your confidence will grow. You will begin to have a bolder approach to fitting into groups because you've learned to listen carefully to the discussion and are able to comment without feeling like the "fifth wheel."

How can you start a conversation? Ask open-ended questions, such as, "How often do you come to these events?" or "How long have you been with your company?" or "What trends are you seeing in your industry?" Stay away from politics and religion... trust me! Telling the story of how you were laid off or how awful your last manager was isn't good form, either. Keep your conversation upbeat and positive. Once you start going down a negative, complaining trail, it's hard to get back on track. The same is true when you are talking to someone who is in a very negative place. People sometimes bring their problems with them to a networking event and spend the entire time telling their stories of how life isn't fair or their family doesn't understand how hard a job search is. Whatever the story, the point is that these people will drag you down with them—harsh, but true. If you sense this is happening, it's perfectly okay to say, "Excuse me, I see someone I need to talk to," and gracefully exit. You don't need to participate in any pity parties. It's a waste of time and energy.

2. BE CONFIDENT PLAY

Being confident takes practice—it is mastering the art of being comfortable in your skin and having trust in yourself. Confidence shows up when you stand up straight and walk with purpose, when you speak the truth yet listen to other points of view. Being confident takes conviction and courage to "put yourself out there" and learn from mistakes. It means taking responsibility for yourself and being accountable for your actions. When you feel fear start taking over, recall your accomplishments and call on your inner strength to calm you down. A little anxiety keeps us on our toes, but overwhelming anxiety paralyzes us. When you start to lose confidence or are overwhelmed, take a deep breath and tell yourself that you are very good at what you do. Remind yourself that you are an accomplished professional with an impressive track record.

Mike is a sales executive who is naturally shy. He'd rather spend time alone and doesn't need other people around him all the time. His introverted personality resisted public speaking, but part of his position required him to give major new product presentations to Fortune 500 CEOs. Mike found that he couldn't sleep the night before these presentations. At times, he'd even be physically ill. He knew he needed to make a change and decided to overcome the fear and anxiety that plagued him.

The first technique Mike used to overcome his fear was to remind himself that he was the expert on the material he was presenting. He also took presentation classes and reviewed his performance by watching videos of his presentations. His practice worked for him! He is still antsy before presentations, but he feels confident. He has a reputation for giving interesting, effective sales presentations, and his sales record reflects success. Here are a few other tips to increase your confidence:

- Take a few moments before you present to calm your mind and visualize yourself being at ease in front of the audience
- Drink warm tea before you give your presentation. Tea helps keep your voice strong and clear.
- Remind yourself that the audience is on your side—they want you to succeed.

3. FOLLOW-UP PHONE CALLS PLAY

One of my clients opened my eyes to the challenge she faced in making follow-up phone calls. She explained that she had no problem meeting people at networking events, but when it came to taking the next step, she didn't know what to say. She knew that getting a handful of business cards at an event wouldn't do her much good if she didn't follow up; however, fear of rejection kept her from making calls. She'd tried email follow-ups, but they weren't very successful. I suggested that she develop a short script and practice making calls with colleagues who would give her feedback.

The follow-up phone call is an often-neglected play. Conducting business strictly via email takes the personal nuances out of communications. Phone calls let your contact hear your voice; they add more personality to your dialogue. Ten years ago, I wouldn't have had to explain the value of hearing someone's voice, because the phone was our main communication tool. Today, many of us hide behind email, but if you use it almost exclusively for communicating, you're missing out.

Before you make a call, think about what you want to say and how you want to say it. A successful call takes into consideration the recipient's time. I always ask if it's a good time for the person to talk. If not, I ask when I can call back. Try standing up while you make the call because it helps you project your voice better. It also puts you in a position of power because chances are the other person is sitting down; visually, you are in command of the conversation. Smile while you're talking. Remind them where you met and quickly tell them what kind of help you're requesting. There are probably going to be action items like making introductions for you or calling people to get names. It's your responsibility to send a follow-up email to the person you've just spoken to, thanking them for taking your call and outlining who has what action items. Send the email as soon as you can after you complete your call. That kind of follow-up doesn't happen very often, so you will leave a good impression; it shows that you're organized and detailed.

4. BE A RESOURCE PLAY

If you want to be a real winner in the career management game, you'll become a reliable resource. You'll listen for what your contacts are interested in and what they need. You'll constantly be on the lookout for articles, websites, and contacts you can send their way. You DON'T KEEP SCORE of who owes you... you just keep giving. The concept of karma is true for this play. In the career game, we need all the good karma we can get.

Helping people make connections makes you a valuable resource. David had been in the job market for fifteen months. During this time, one of the projects he undertook was to start his own public relations company. It was an income stream for him while he searched for a full-time position. He did contract work for former clients and referrals, and because he talked to vendors and suppliers, he saw sales opportunities and recommended his clients for various projects. He established himself as a trusted intermediary. As a result, David had no problem getting the recommendations that eventually landed him a new position. Follow David's example by listening and remembering what your contacts' challenges are. As you grow your network, keep on the lookout for vendors, consultants, etc., who can help your contacts. Keep these people on file and make introductions regularly. Your contacts will know they can count on you to refer them to great resources; in the process, you will have become a great resource yourself—and grown your reputation both within and outside your own field.

5. LIVING YOUR BRAND PLAY

Living your brand means that you take ownership of your values and talents. You read your vision and mission statements regularly, and you showcase your talents every chance you get. For instance, Joan's brand is a "trendsetter and early adopter of technology for small financial service business growth." Joan's business introduces applications to financial service business owners to help increase their bottom line. Her team tries out new applications to make sure they have all the functionality they need, so she can speak from real-life experience. Joan is the expert on what major challenges face her clients and recommends solutions for them. She lives her brand by continuously educating herself about what's new and where the industry is headed. She sends out regular marketing and informational emails regarding new technology, and what she has discovered is that her clients share her monthly emails with *their* clients. By living her brand, she has a built-in sales referral source.

6. SIX DEGREES OF SEPARATION PLAY

Under the theory of six degrees of separation, we're all just six people apart from the person we want to meet. That places a high priority on making and cultivating our connections, and it's a play that really works.

Ever since I was a kid, for example, I wanted to do a radio show. A couple of years ago, I decided I'd try to see how long it would take to make the radio show a reality. The answer was "not long." I tapped into my network and found that a friend of mine had been doing a show for several years—and it turned out she was always looking for guests to interview! I co-hosted with her for a few months and had a great time. Here's how you can master the six degrees of separation for your playbook:

— Decide whom you want to meet and why.
— Determine exactly what you'll say when you meet your target person.

— Make it a point to tell everyone you talk to for the *next month* that you want to meet this person. Ask your connections if they know your target person or if they could put you in contact with someone who can get you closer to meeting the person you want to meet. You'll be amazed who knows whom and what a small world it really is.

Let's review how the six plays you just learned about work in the real world. These are stories about clients who used the plays to move their searches forward.

JIM'S STORY

Jim is a marketing executive who has been in the hospitality industry with a leading hotel chain for fifteen years. He is well known for his marketing savvy and successful campaigns... so you can imagine Jim's surprise when he was called into his boss' office one week before Thanksgiving and told that his position was being eliminated. Jim had heard about a possible restructuring within his division. What he didn't know was that the head of the division had accepted a new position and was leaving the company. His exit led to a major restructure, and Jim was out.

I met Jim shortly after his layoff. His attitude was great. He had already started to contact his network and spread the word that he was back in the market (Six Degrees of Separation Play). Another avenue Jim wanted to explore was the independent contractor arena. We developed a search plan for him that included looking for a full-time position *while* building an independent consulting business (Living Your Brand Play). Jim decided to spend sixty percent of his time on the full-time activities and forty percent on the consulting side. He set a ninety-day timeframe to review his results.

By the end of three months, Jim had two consulting contracts and no solid job offers. He liked the freedom he had as a consultant, and the fees were covering his expenses, so Jim cut back on the time he spent looking for a full-time position but kept his network updated and active (Networking Play). His consulting business thrived. What he learned was that he needed to keep his network active and his eye open for opportunities in the marketplace. He now understands firsthand how quickly situations can change and how to react when they do.

—————————————————————————————— **MARK'S STORY ⟩**

I met Mark at the community career center where I volunteer. He came in as client looking for a business development position with an advertising agency. He had been in advertising for the last seven years and, prior to that, was in the marketing department for a large media company. I helped him revamp his resume, and we started talking about how he could quickly increase his network. I suggested he volunteer at the center. This would give him access to job listings and exposure to corporations in the area through the job posting process.

Mark took my advice and became a volunteer. He also got involved with the board of directors in fundraising for the center (Be a Resource Play). In this role, he was able to meet CEOs and CFOs he could add to his network (Networking Play). Mark's goal was to establish himself as an exceptional business development professional by growing the number of contributions the center received from local businesses (Be Confident Play). He was able to increase funding by forty percent. Because of this success, he was recognized by the career center as its top volunteer, and he caught the attention of business leaders who helped him get a marketing position with a new technology company in the area (Six Degrees of Separation Play).

Mark's job search took several months, lots of hard work, and commitment. There were times when he wondered how volunteering and "giving his time away" would help. However, he would quickly stop those thoughts and realize he was actively job searching and that volunteering was an essential piece of his strategy. Mark is now the president of the board of directors for the center. He continues to educate business leaders about the center's value and why it's a good investment.

──────────────────────── **BRIAN'S STORY ↘**

Brian was an editor at a major publishing house undergoing huge changes. The world of books was spinning between traditional techniques and new online self-publishing shops and e-books. Brian knew his industry was rapidly changing but hadn't taken the steps necessary to understand its market needs. He had been hiding in his cubicle, hoping that the rumors about technology and sending jobs offshore would magically disappear.

Originally, Brian thought he could wait it out and see what would happen—that his company would embrace technology so his job would remain intact. After two years of waiting and watching the company decline, Brian lost his job. It was at that point that he realized his skills were becoming outdated. He started attending workshops, which is where I met Brian. I was giving a personal branding workshop, and he stayed after the session to talk to me and find out how we could leverage our connections to help each other (Networking Play). He told me that he had worked for a major newspaper as a sports reporter and had transitioned into publishing when the paper cut back on reporters. He said he felt like he was running from technology because jobs were being gobbled up by applications that turned everyday people into on-the-spot reporters. He knew he couldn't change this trend, so he needed to figure out how to make his experience work for him.

As we talked, I began to realize that Brian would be a good fit in a corporate communications division. He had a reporter's sense for getting at the bottom of a situation quickly and could communicate thoughts well. His listening and writing skills were great, and he showcased his work in a weekly blog (Living Your Brand Play). Because part of Brian's challenge in the past was setting unrealistic goals, we had a goal-setting meeting to create a solid and feasible plan. We also adapted his ability to meet story deadlines to meeting deadlines for his job search.

For the search, Brian focused on ten target companies, using the following categories to narrow it down:

- Company size
- Product/service lines
- Challenges faced
- Brian's expertise
- Total compensation
- Corporate culture
- Company connections, if any

One obvious category is missing: a job posting. Brian did not make that one of his primary concerns because he felt he would be eliminating target companies that didn't currently have open positions. He also knew that organizations have positions that may not be posted immediately, and this was a chance Brian was willing take. He began communicating with a college friend who worked for a consumer goods company. His friend then introduced him to the manager of the corporate communications department (Six Degrees of Separation Play). During their meeting, Brian had the confidence to answer the manager honestly when he asked Brian how he liked the company's website (Be Confident Play). Brian explained that the website needed to be reworked because it was dated and didn't give clients the perception of a cutting-edge organization. Brian's plays paid off for him several months later: He was hired into the corporate communications department of that same company.

Consider these six plays as the basics you'll need to begin developing your own scrimmages, customized for your unique goals, experiences, and career. Practice them often—challenge yourself, for example, to play all six moves in one week—and you WILL see that scoreboard light up.

And speaking of scoreboard, a game is not a game if there is no way to measure performance! The next chapter will teach you how to keep score and track your progress throughout the career game—and for life. Ready to see how you're doing?

CHAPTER EIGHT

PERFORMANCE MEASUREMENT – KEEPING SCORE

IN many ways, keeping score and measuring your performance is the most exciting part of the career game, because you get to see your progress on a daily basis. Setting and meeting your goals builds your confidence and gives you the energy to keep going, especially when the search gets difficult.

Reviewing your vision and mission daily and implementing your marketing plan are essential to your success. However, your vision itself can be very daunting—even overwhelming at times. This is when those little voices go off in your head and warn you that your vision is too big, not reachable, and that you don't deserve it. When this happens, and it will, take your vision and break it up into "bite-sized pieces" so you can manage it. We refer to these pieces as goals. After all, if your goal is to win the Super Bowl, you take it one game at a time. You then break the game down to one play at a time.

There's a very practical method that I used to set goals and follow through. It's called S.M.A.R.T. goal setting, and it stands for:

Specific
Measurable
Attainable
Realistic
Timely

Often we set ourselves up for disappointment because we set unreasonable goals. When we don't reach them, we feel like failures. We usually don't realize that if our goals had been more reasonable, they'd also be more attainable. Let's look at how this works in real life.

One classic example is setting a weight loss goal. I usually start with wanting to lose twenty pounds; that's my goal, but I'm not very specific about how or when I plan to do this. Let's see how this goal stacks up against our S.M.A.R.T. goals model. It's specific and measurable: twenty pounds. Here's where it gets tricky, though. Is the goal attainable? How realistic is it? Most importantly, is it timely? In other words, is there a date set when these twenty pounds magically disappear? No. There's no date.

I don't know about you, but losing one pound a week is realistic for me. At that rate, it would take five months to lose twenty pounds. Okay, then, let's rewrite the goal based on more realistic information and add a timeframe.

> **Goal**: To lose twenty pounds in the next five months. That's specific, measurable, attainable, realistic, and timely. The last step is to create a daily plan to meet my goal. In this example, it might include joining Weight Watchers or some organization that offers structure and discipline, or any plan including regular exercise and calorie intake measurements. The important thing is that the plan is *written* and results are measured.

Let's review how goal setting plays out in the job search game. One of my clients, Rachel, is a nurse whose hospital was facing budget problems. Rachel was one of the first to be laid off.

Rachel had known the layoff was coming, so she had put together her plan: She aimed to attain a new director of nursing position at one of five area hospitals in six months. With a goal set, Rachel was ready to execute. However, one of her biggest challenges was to stay focused, so she developed a daily action item checklist. She followed the S.M.A.R.T. goal setting method and created a form to keep track of her activities. She set goals for herself and developed daily tasks. As she completed them, she checked them off her list. By the end of each week, she had met her smaller goals, which kept her focused on the big end result.

Her daily goals were in line with her vision: to educate patients so they could live better lives. Her mission statement was: to create a patient wellness program that is proactive and measurable. Rachel knew that when patients change their eating habits and add exercise to their daily routine, they see dramatic, positive changes in their weight, blood pressure, and moods.

Here's a list that Rachel created of action items she needed to complete to reach her vision. She started out at a high level and then drilled down two levels for each action item so she could get to the details. Her list looked like this:

GOALS FOR THE WEEK

1 Develop a list of top ten hospitals
— Create a contact list

2 Increase network by two new contacts
— Ask existing network for names
— Schedule face-to-face meetings

3 Contact one healthcare recruiter
— Create a list of top ten recruiters
— Schedule meeting with one recruiter

4 Create new resume

PERFORMANCE MEASUREMENT – KEEPING SCORE

Rachel knew that when she was under stress she needed to exercise and quiet her mind through meditation. She believed in feeding her body and her soul, so she included working out and meditating in her daily activities. Her daily log looked like this:

JOB SEARCH DAILY CHECKLIST: ACTION ITEMS

DAY 1 – GOAL

Work out for 60 minutes	Completed
Attend healthcare networking event	Done – send resume to two new contacts
Meditate for 15 minutes	Completed
Revamp resume	Completed
Complete Hot Jobs profile	Completed

DAY 2 – GOAL

Work out for 60 minutes	Completed
Meet with new contact James Edward	Done – send Chris new resume
Meet with recruiter Mary Savory	Completed
Meditate for 15 minutes	Completed
Research Edwards Hospital	Completed – contact HR manager

DAY 3 – GOAL

Work out for 60 minutes	Completed
Complete LinkedIn profile	Completed
Meet with John – ask for referrals	Done – follow up with Mike and John Marino
Meditate for 15 minutes	Completed
Attend networking event	Don – follow up with Pam and Chuck Echter

DAY 4 – GOAL

Work out for 60 minutes	Done
Meet with healthcare recruiter Rita DeWulf	Done – follow up with Tim
Meditate for 15 minutes	Don't have time
Create list of area hospitals	Completed
Post resume on three job websites	Done – schedule date to renew postings

DAY 5 – GOAL

Work out for 60 minutes	Done
Meditate for 15 minutes	Done
Create hospital contact list	Not completed – schedule for next week
Create action items for next week	Done
Make two follow-up calls	Completed

Rachel's checklist had room for notes and comments so that she remembered what her follow-up items were. If she didn't complete a task, she could remind herself to reschedule it. Using a simple checklist helped Rachel stay on track. She met all of her goals for the week with the exception of creating a list of hospital contacts. She simply scheduled it for the next week and felt great about what she had accomplished.

Rachel is now the director of nursing at one of her target hospitals. She is well on her way to fulfilling her vision and mission because she was able to sell senior management on her idea of developing a proactive program to educate patients about nutrition and exercise. She admits that if she hadn't kept track of her daily accomplishments, she wouldn't be where she is today. Rachel discovered that she could make her vision and mission reality by measuring her performance.

It's surprising how many people forget the performance measurement part of the game. It isn't enough to create your vision and mission statements and complete your marketing plan. Unless you execute and produce results, you're not really in the game. Keeping score helps you answer the most important question: **Are you accomplishing what you set out to accomplish?** Remember that you are the product. You are the marketer. You must hold yourself accountable.

Why is holding ourselves accountable so hard to do? Because we don't want to admit to ourselves that we've failed to deliver on our promises. We can become our own worst enemies when we start to fudge and make excuses for not following through. Here is a list of some common excuses I've come across:

"I need to mow the lawn before I make follow-up phone calls."

"My son had a baseball game this afternoon and I had to be there to watch him. I didn't have time to go to a networking event."

"My wife gave me a list of things to do around the house, so I'll complete those before I start my job search."

"I needed to clean the house from top to bottom, so I didn't send out my resume like I said I would."

The real reason we don't follow through is usually fear. Fear of rejection. Fear of humiliation. But when you take responsibility and record your daily activities in a log like Rachel's, you'll see whether or not you're performing. You can't fool yourself for too long.

PERFORMANCE MAINTENANCE

As you reach your daily, weekly, and long-term goals, don't stop setting new ones. In a new position, you'll have corporate goals to meet. Don't forget to set personal career goals as well; goals like maintaining and increasing your network, becoming involved in industry associations, and learning new skills will serve you well. Chances are good that you'll find yourself in job search mode again at some point, and this time you'll have your plan, your team, your winning plays, and a no-fail goal measurement system!

AFTERWORD: TAKE BACK YOUR POWER

❝ Leadership is a matter of having people look at you and gain confidence in seeing how you react. If you're in control, they're in control. ❞

—TOM LANDRY

CONGRATULATIONS! If you've made it to this point, you've learned all about the new career game and how to play it—and win. You've created your vision and mission statements, begun thinking of and marketing yourself as a brand, discovered how to network for life, and put together your winning team and plays. In other words, you're well on your way to reclaiming your career *and* your personal power. How does it feel to be in charge?

Be very proud of yourself. It takes courage and discipline to look honestly at what choices you make and how they affect you. Throughout this process, you may have discovered some things about yourself that need to be changed. Maybe you've settled for second best in your career. Maybe you haven't been living according to your values. Or maybe you realized you have no passion for the career you're in. Whatever your situation, pat yourself on the back and celebrate your courage—you've looked your setbacks in the eye and come out the other side a stronger, more well-informed version of yourself. A winner.

Throughout this book, I've used the stories of people I've worked with to illustrate strategies and show that you're not alone in playing the new career game. As a concluding note, I want to share several more stories of people who underwent job loss and career transitions and, like you, came out on top.

Roger is a financial executive who "fell" into his profession. He started out working for an insurance company and set his sights on working his way to the top ranks. He took a detour when one of his former managers told him about a position with a new company. The salary and benefits were considerably greater than he was making. In addition, the company was much smaller, so his climb to the top wouldn't take as long.

Roger took the job and soon discovered that the position he had been promised was about to change, because the company needed to provide a new client with customized services. Roger was assigned to head this new project team. He learned new laws and regulations about corporate investments.

For twenty-five years, Roger was the leading expert in his field. He was also about to be laid off. He didn't see the job loss coming. When he was notified that his position had been eliminated, he decided to take a few months off and used this time to assess where he wanted to take his career and life. He had always been interested in teaching at the college level, so he took a risk and applied for an adjunct teaching position. He was accepted.

Roger discovered how fulfilling teaching was for him. He also discovered that he couldn't live on the salary, so he had two choices: get another position in the industry he'd been in or think outside the box and figure out how to make a good living in the education field. He asked me to help him put together a personal marketing strategy so he could reach his goal. As part of his plan, we created a team of experts who would hold him accountable. One of the members of his team was a financial expert who helped Roger budget his money and downsize so he could make his career transition. Roger now has several revenue streams, including consulting, teaching, and writing. Specifically, Roger is a contractor for a consulting firm, so he's on an "as needed" basis. The consulting assignments may be for three days or three months. Roger also teaches an MBA series twice a year as an adjunct professor at his local university. And finally, Roger writes articles for two associations he belongs to. These are paid writing assignments.

Roger used the personal marketing strategies I taught him to successfully sell himself as a consultant, teacher, and writer. He made contacts and connections through his network to get the introductions he needed at the consulting firms, universities, and associations. These assignments didn't happen overnight or sequentially. The teaching gig came first because Roger had several solid contacts who made personal introductions for him. Then one of his students told him about a consulting firm that was looking for consultants; that was his introduction into the world of consulting. Roger's biggest challenge now is juggling availability with demand. He has learned to be on the lookout for other income producing opportunities.

RITA'S STORY ➋

This is one of my favorite stories because it reflects how stamina and believing in yourself pays off. Rita started her career as a receptionist. She knew that she would need a college degree if she wanted to move into her dream career as a financial analyst. Rita took advantage of her employer's education loans and finally earned her degree eight years later. I met Rita at a networking event shortly after she'd graduated, and her enthusiasm and positive attitude were contagious. While she was working toward her degree, she had been promoted into the finance department. Rita took on any and all projects, including developing a thorough procedures manual for the company. She felt on top of the world. Then her company was bought by a competitor. There were redundancies, so many financial positions were eliminated—including Rita's. She was totally unprepared for the layoff.

Rita had kept my card from the time we'd met at the networking event. She contacted me and explained her situation. She had made a list of all the activities she felt needed to be completed to begin her job search. However, when I asked her what position she wanted she said, "I'll take anything. I just need a job!" The enthusiasm I had seen in Rita when we'd first met was totally gone, replaced by bitterness and desperation. These emotions are natural when things don't go the way we expect. Her challenge now was to not only to find another position, but

AFTERWORD: TAKE BACK YOUR POWER

also to get her head on straight. Rita was living in "pity city" and she needed to change addresses.

Our first project was to work on her attitude. She needed to quickly deal with her negative feelings and move into a more positive state of mind. I asked Rita to detail her accomplishments and to give herself credit for what she'd contributed to the organization. I also asked her to contact five people she knew well (excluding family) who would tell her what her strengths were. This is a very effective exercise to build up self-confidence and begin the process of believing in oneself again. Rita was blaming herself for staying at the company as long as she had before it was sold, but the fact is that the company would have been sold no matter what Rita did. Her grieving was very personal and draining all her energy. I coached her to go from a "coulda, shoulda, woulda" mentality to an "I can, I am, and I will" frame of mind. We worked on her resume and held practice interviews. We also developed a marketing plan for her with aggressive completion dates so that she would stay focused on her job search. Rita began to understand that one of her assets was her loyalty; however, she also learned that she was loyal to a fault and could now understand that being loyal doesn't mean needing to go down with the ship! She learned that she had to be loyal to *herself* first and make the best decisions for her career and life. It wasn't easy for Rita to turn herself around, but she did. She now has a new position where she can see her contributions to the organization.

LOU'S STORY ↴

My client, Lou, had a reputation for being hard to work with. He had started working in the technology industry in its infancy. It was a cutthroat, aggressive environment and Lou thrived on it. Lou always made his sales numbers, but his people skills were lacking and he knew it. His company eliminated his position, and by the time I met him, he'd been in transition for four months. His reputation was well known in the technology industry, and it was eliminating him from interviews. Lou wanted to change his image to a more personable, mature, customer-oriented Lou. We really had our work cut out for us!

Our first step was to develop a marketing strategy to introduce Lou as a subject matter expert and top sales talent. Lou wrote the following marketing plan:

——— LOU'S MARKETING PLAN ———

Vision Statement: I will teach sales people to be more efficient in their jobs and increase their sales.

Mission Statement: I will be a resource and expert of sales management software and provide unheard-of customer service.

Branding Statement: I am THE expert in sales management software. If you want the best in product and service, come to me.

Features: innovative, results-driven, forward-thinking, strategic, powerful network.

Benefits: generate sales consistently, add to bottom line, streamline the sales process.

After Lou completed his marketing plan, he started calling his former managers and asking them how he could repair his reputation for being hard to work with. Two of his contacts told him that he would have to prove to the market that he had changed. The third manager decided to give Lou another chance, so he was hired on a three-month sales contract.

On the job, Lou proved that he had changed by controlling his temper and being more patient. This company also had Lou work with a coach who helped Lou begin to notice what events would trigger his temper. For instance, Lou would go ballistic if anyone was late for a meeting—no exceptions. He needed to understand that everyone wasn't on "Lou time," and he learned to cut people some slack. Lou did an excellent job during the contract phase and is now a full-time employee. He told me later that the exercise of writing out his marketing plan helped him see that his good points were being overshadowed by his glaring temper issues. Talking to his former managers was a humbling experience that gave him a second chance. Now Lou is back at the top of his game and doing well.

These stories, and the others in this book, all have common threads: They are about people finding the courage to believe in themselves. They are about people who faced challenges and obstacles and successfully overcame them by developing a strategy to reach their career goals. They learned to remain marketable, keep their skills updated, stay open to new concepts and technology, develop their networks, and—crucially—understand the rules of the new career game. Now that you're equipped with the knowledge and tools you need to win, enter the game with confidence. Success is only a few plays away!

If you want to talk to me directly about the book or your career, please contact me at jan.highgainco@gmail.com. I look forward to hearing from you!

RESOURCES

To give you even more of a leg up in the game, here are a few websites and books my clients and I have found helpful throughout the career transition process. Enjoy exploring what they have to offer!

WEBSITES

www.danpink.com – Dan Pink's website is a great source for information on careers and business. He has a real grasp on what's going on in the world of work.

www.damngood.com/jobseekers/tips.html – Great FAQ and tips on creating a winning resume.

www.knockemdead.com – Martin Yates is THE resume expert, and his website is packed with tips and templates for job seekers.

www.quintcareers.com/job-seeker_checklists.html – This site has everything job seekers need and more.

www.reCareered.com – Innovative search tips, great blogs, and informative online workshops, as well as timely career and job market information.

BOOKS

Wake-up Calls – Eric Allenbaugh

Excuses Begone! – Wayne Dyer

Career Renegade – Jonathan Fields

What Would Google Do? – Jeff Jarvis

Complete Idiot's Guide to Branding Yourself – Sherry & Ray Paprocki

Influencer – The Power to Change Anything – Kerry Patterson, Joseph Grenny

Brain Rules – John Medina

The Brand Called You – Peter Montoya with Tim Vandehey

Driven – Daniel Pink

Free Agent Nation – Daniel Pink

Strength Finder 2.0 – Tom Rath

www.ingramcontent.com/pod-product-compliance
Lightning Source LLC
Chambersburg PA
CBHW050553210326

41521CB00008B/951